SAINT AUGUSTINE'S

Conversion

GARRY WILLS

SAINT AUGUSTINE'S
Conversion

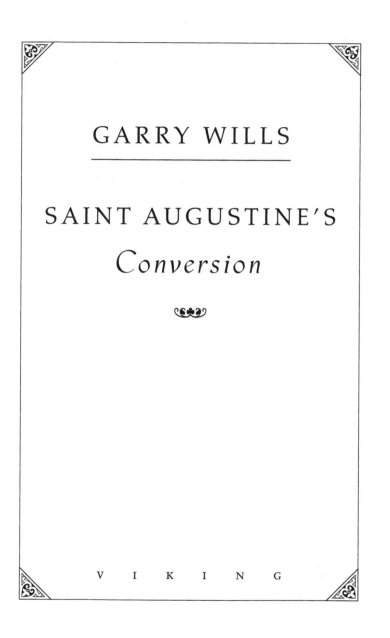

VIKING

VIKING
Published by the Penguin Group
Penguin Group (USA) Inc., 375 Hudson Street, New York, New York 10014, U.S.A.
Penguin Group (Canada), 10 Alcorn Avenue, Toronto, Ontario, Canada M4V 3B2
    (a division of Pearson Penguin Canada Inc.)
Penguin Books Ltd, 80 Strand, London WC2R 0RL, England
Penguin Ireland, 25 St Stephen's Green, Dublin 2, Ireland (a division of Penguin Books Ltd)
Penguin Group (Australia), 250 Camberwell Road, Camberwell,
    Victoria 3124, Australia (a division of Pearson Australia Group Pty Ltd)
Penguin Books India Pvt Ltd, 11 Community Centre, Panchsheel Park,
    New Delhi - 110 017, India
Penguin Group (NZ), cnr Airborne and Rosedale Roads, Albany,
    Auckland, New Zealand (a division of Pearson New Zealand Ltd)
Penguin Books (South Africa) (Pty) Ltd, 24 Sturdee Avenue, Rosebank,
    Johannesburg 2196, South Africa
Penguin Books Ltd, Registered Offices: 80 Strand, London WC2R 0RL, England

First published in 2004 by Viking Penguin,
a member of Penguin Group (USA) Inc.

10 9 8 7 6 5 4 3 2 1

LIBRARY OF CONGRESS CATALOGING IN PUBLICATION DATA

Augustine, Saint, Bishop of Hippo.
    [Confessiones. Liber 8. English]
    Saint Augustine's conversion / [introduction and commentary by] Garry Wills.
        p. cm.
    ISBN 0-670-03352-9
    1. Augustine, Saint, Bishop of Hippo.   2. Christian saints—Algeria—Hippo
    (Extinct city)—Biography.   3. Conversion—Christianity.   I. Wills, Garry,
    1934– II. Title.

    BR65.A6E5 2004
    270.2'092—dc22   2004053585

This book is printed on acid-free paper. ∞
Printed in the United States of America
Set in Aldus with Phaistos display and MT Arabesque Ornaments
Designed by Carla Bolte

TO PHIL BERRIGAN

gone but with us

CONTENTS

Key to Brief Citations

Boldface numerals in square brackets **[20]** refer to paragraphs in Book Eight of *The Testimony*.

[*comm.*] refers to the Commentary (p. 107).

O, with volume and page (e.g., O 2.52–53), refers to James J. O'Donnell, *Augustine, "Confessions"* (Oxford University Press, 1992).

T, with book and paragraph number (e.g., T 10.5), refers to books of *The Testimony* other than Book Eight.

I translate all Scripture texts from the Latin versions Augustine used. The Psalms are numbered as in the Vulgate Latin Bible and in the Douay-Rheims Catholic translation of them.

SAINT AUGUSTINE'S

Conversion

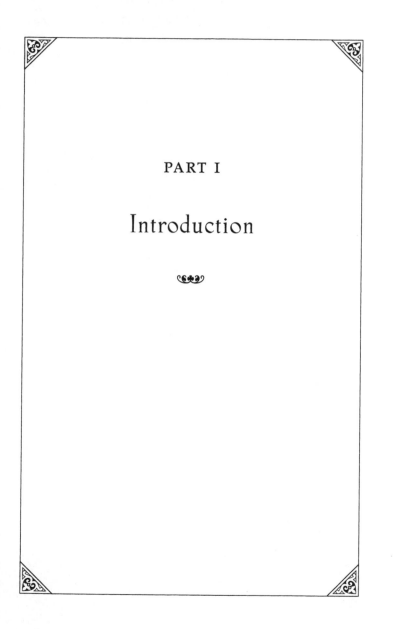

PART I

Introduction

1. The Book of Conversions

Book Eight of *The Testimony* tells the second most famous religious conversion story in Western literature, second only to that of Saint Paul, on which it is modeled. These two accounts have jointly determined much of what has been thought and written on the whole subject of conversion—in such classics on the subject as William James's *The Varieties of Religious Experience* (1902) or Arthur Darby Nock's *Conversion* (1933). The stories of Paul and Augustine have led to a belief that "real" conversion is sudden, effected by the incursion of an outside force, and emotionally wrenching. Certainly Augustine does everything he can to create that image in the emotional paroxysm of the garden scene that closes Book Eight. He prepares for that moment by an elaborate arrangement of conversion stories—seven of them, with his own coming as the climactic eighth case, and with Paul's as a ninth one implicit in the text that Augustine reads in the garden. The artistry of Augustine's presentation as well as the gripping nature of its contents has made Book Eight the most famous and most cited book in *The Testimony*. Among other things, it contains the most frequently cited sentence—"Lord, give me chastity and self-control, but not just now" [17].

But what does conversion mean here? We often use the word to indicate the adoption of a new religion. One is a Jewish convert, or a Muslim convert. But Augustine tells us he had accepted the Christian faith before he went into the garden. He already believed in the basic doctrines of the church [1, 18]. In fact, only one of the conversion stories he uses involves the acceptance of a new creed, and that one, exceptionally, is not recounted to Augustine by another person but inserted by him into one such reported story. This tale-within-a-tale (of Sergius Paul's conversion at Acts 12.6–12) is used to show that celebrity conversions are worth encouraging. Everyone else "converted" here was already a Christian in belief, and most of them (Anthony, the four in Trier) were not only doctrinal believers but had been baptized. The only such "convert" who had not been baptized is the subject of the first and longest story, about Victorinus, who was a believer though he did not want to sacrifice his worldly position by open profession of Christianity. His is a baptism story, and the story is expressly told to Augustine (by Simplician) to make him give up worldly ties by undergoing baptism.

With the exception of this baptism story, the other conversion narratives are more properly vocation narratives, telling how a person already Christian (and already baptized) receives a higher calling—to the monastic life (Pontician's friends) or to a hermit's life (Anthony). Augustine has chosen his parallel narratives carefully, since his own case will combine both kinds of spiritual change—he will come not only to accept baptism, but to undertake a further commitment, to celibacy. These are separate matters, as Augustine tells his mother in reporting the garden struggle's outcome. He reports that her prayers have been rewarded beyond her own expectation. She had wanted him, when she had a dream about him (T 3.19), to be converted from Manicheism to Christianity, joining her on the ruler's edge of belief in Jesus. He now tells her that the garden experience has gone beyond the conversion she prayed for, giving him the further call to celibacy [20]. This is more properly a vocation story than a conversion one—which is why he chose six of his seven parallel narratives from people already converted to the faith.

Of course, conversion in the broad sense does not necessarily entail a change of creed. It can refer to any significant spiritual reorientation (whether sudden or gradual). In that sense, Augustine's life up to the garden scene was one long tale of conversions—from Christianity to Manicheism, from Manicheism to a Ciceronian Skepticism, from Skepticism to Materialism, from Materialism to Neoplatonism, and from Neoplatonism to Christianity. None of these breaks was absolutely clean. As a Skeptic, he still felt a need for the savor of Christ's name (T 5.25), something that had retained its hold on him from the time when he begged for baptism during a childhood sickness (T 1.17). And he would always retain a Manichean sense of the struggle with evil (O 3.48). The Christianity he embraced in Milan retained for a long time as many Neoplatonic as gospel elements. "The conversions of Augustine were many, and they did not end in the garden in Milan" (O 1.xlii). There was as much continuity as disjunction in his life's development—which makes the clean break described in Book Eight so striking by its contrast with what went before.

It is a contrast striking enough that one must ask whether Augustine has not, for theological or other purpose, exaggerated its suddenness and violence. This suspicion is reinforced by the conflict between what he was writing, in or near Milan, at the time of his conversion and what he tells us, over ten years later, in Book Eight. The garden story has long been doubted—at least from 1888, when Boissier and Harnack challenged it, and that has involved Book Eight in controversy. It is hard to sort out all the problems of the book because so many of us first approached it with presuppositions derived from what we knew, or thought we knew, or had been told, about Augustine's life and conversion. There are many myths that have accumulated around this subject. In calling them myths I do not claim that they lack truth of some order—just what kind and degree of order will be the matter for decision—but that they do not give a literal report of what was happening or being thought at the time being described. There are at least four such myths—that of Monnica, that of Ambrose, that of Paul at Damascus, and that of Augustine in the garden. In order, then:

2. The Myth of Monnica[1]

His mother joined him at Milan, and he was
under the influence of her life and faith . . .
—Nock, *Conversion*

It is often assumed or asserted that Augustine's conversion was the result of his mother's efforts and prayers. It is true that by the time Augustine wrote *The Testimony*, he attributed his conversion to God's grace, and attributed much of that grace to Monnica's prayers. But the idea that she had a controlling influence at the time, or even a very strong one, cannot be substantiated in the natural order, or by any literal reading of the evidence. The hagiographical approach to her life has greatly inflated her role—yet all that we know of her comes from *The Testimony*, which does not present her as a perfect mother or Christian. The exaggeration of her influence reaches a dark apogee in Rebecca West's biography of Augustine:

> She did not want her son to grow up. . . . It was fortunate that in her religion she had a perfect and, indeed, noble instrument for obtaining her desire that her son should not become a man. Very evidently Christianity need not mean emasculation, but the long struggles of Augustine and Monnica imply that in his case it did. . . . With her smooth competence she must have been able to make the Church a most alluring prospect.[2]

The most significant thing Augustine says of his mother during his own youth was that she had fled from the epicenter of Babylon (worldly corruption) but was loitering *(tardior ibat)* in other parts of it (T 2.8), which is not the definition of a saint, by his own exacting standards. He rebukes Monnica for worldliness on several occasions—when she did not baptize him after his childhood sickness (T 1.18), when she did not urge marriage on him earlier (T 2.8), when she arranged a worldly marriage to an underage heiress (T 6.23). She was far from controlling his life. He ignored her advice on sexual continence, saying he would have blushed to obey words he considered "womanish" (T 2.7). He remained a Manichean for a decade despite her objections. He lied in order to give her the slip before leaving Africa (T 5.15). He mentions her name only once (T 9.37) in all his five million words of writings.

He did not initially share her admiration for Ambrose, the bishop of Milan who would baptize him. He did not join her in the church when Ambrose held his long vigil of defiance against the empress Justina (T 9.15). He did not, at that point, believe in church miracles (as opposed to gospel miracles), and he no doubt differed with her on Ambrose's theatrical introduction of miracle-working martyrs' bodies into his fight with the empress (T 9.15).[3] This attitude toward miracles would not have made him well-disposed to his mother's claim that she could tell divine visions by their odor (T 6.23). Nor would he have sympathized with her semi-Manichean rites at martyrs' tombs, from which she would not have desisted but for her reverence toward Ambrose (T 6.2).

These misgivings, no doubt stronger at the time than when he records them a decade later, are countered, of course, by the marvelous tribute he pays to Monnica in Book Nine of *The Testimony*. But that tribute follows on his rediscovery of Monnica at Cassiciacum, just before his baptism, when for the first time she was included in the discussions of his philosophical friends. Before this, he had the prejudice of his time and class against the intellects of women. His first plan of a philosophical community, formed in Milan, fell through over the issue of including women (T 6.24). O'Donnell suggests that Monnica may have been illiterate (O 3.115). Monnica at first resisted her inclusion in the Cassiciacum discussions, but Augustine encouraged her.[4] He laughed with surprise at her earthy wisdom, on this first occasion of her displaying it to him.[5] He tells her, "I am daily struck anew by your natural ability."[6] The sexist compliment he pays her is itself revealing: "Forgetting her sex, we almost thought that some important man had joined us."[7]

On the basis of his new respect for Monnica, the mystical experience he shared with this unlettered woman (as first reported a decade later from his bishop's residence) is meant to destroy the presumption that soul-culture demands exercise in the liberal arts—though he continued to hold that view for some time after the reported experience. Monnica did not lead him to baptism. Rather, baptism led him to Monnica. The long excursus on her in Book Nine is very likely derived from a eulogy composed first for the benefit of her children and grandchildren. We know how much his own son loved his grandmother (T 9.29). Presumably, Augustine's sister and brother had the same feeling for her, as did his brother's children. If, as Courcelle plausibly maintained, Augustine could write the tribute to Alypius (T 6.11–16) for Paulinus of Nola, surely he could have done the same for his own relatives.[8] Augustine only realized her worth in Monnica's last months, after his conversion—for which she was not responsible, except by prayer.

3. The Myth of Ambrose

... he was under the influence of her life and faith,
as well as of Ambrose's sermons.
—Nock, *Conversion*

It is a commonplace that Ambrose, presiding in Milan, played the key role in Augustine's conversion, mainly by showing him that the Jewish scripture, which had seemed crude, could be read symbolically. Ambrose's sermons are supposed to have brought about this change in attitude. But Augustine tells us that he listened to the sermons for their style, not their content, and that he thought the style inferior to that of Faustus the Manichean (T 5.23). Far from opening the scripture to him, Ambrose just recommended that he read Isaiah *after* Augustine told him he was already willing to be baptized—and Augustine, far from reading Isaiah symbolically, found the book impenetrable (T 9.13). Augustine found what he needed with the help of Simplician, who directed him to the New Testament, to the letters of Paul, which would play a key role in the garden. Ambrose was still a distant and useless figure when Augustine underwent what he describes in that garden:

He [Ambrose] was unaware of my seethings at the pit of peril. I could not inquire of him what I wished, crowded out as I was from his hearing and speaking by a swarm of those with worldly needs, to whose demands he gave his attention (T 6.3).

Except for brief interviews on business, there was clearly no occasion to pursue fully all that I desired from that oracle of yours, his breast. To pour out my needs would have taken up time that was simply not available (T 6.4).

Those passages are enough to refute the old idea that Augustine was referring to Ambrose when he wrote his Neoplatonist mentor, Mallius Theodore, about "conversations held with you and our priest friend" *(presbyter noster).*[9] The man referred to is clearly Simplician, Ambrose's Neoplatonist teacher, who baptized Ambrose and succeeded him as bishop of Milan. Augustine went to him for spiritual guidance. He corresponded with Simplician in later years (Epistle 37), something that Augustine never did with Ambrose.[10] It was as the doyen of Milan Neoplatonists that Simplician would have known and conversed with Theodore. And Theodore, to whom *The Testament* makes only glancing and denigrating reference (T 7.13), is described by Augustine, when he was at Cassiciacum, as a leading force in his conversion and Christian aspirations.[11]

Since, my Theodore, I look only to you for what I need, impressed by your possession of it, consider what type of man is presented to you, what state I believe I am in, what kind of help I am sure you can give me. . . . I came to recognize, in the conversations about God held with you and our priest friend, that He is not to be considered as in any way corporeal. . . . After I read a few books of Plotinus, of whom you are a devotee, and tested them against the standard of the sacred writings, I was on fire. . . . So I beg you by your own goodness, by your concern for others, by the linkage and interaction of our souls, stretch out your hand to me—to love me and believe you are loved in return and held dear. If I beg this, I may, helped by my own poor effort, reach the happiness in this life that I suspect you have already gained. That you may know what I am doing, how I am conducting my friends to shelter, and that you may see in this my very soul (for I have no other means to reveal it to you), I thought I should address you and should dedicate in your name this early discourse, which I consider more religious than my other ones, and therefore worthy of you. Its subject is appropriate, since together we pondered the subject of happiness in this life, and I hold no gift of God could be greater than that. I am not abashed by your eloquence (why should that abash me which, without rivaling it, I honor) nor by the loftiness of your position—however great it is, you discountenance it, knowing that only what one masters can turn a truly favorable countenance on one.[12]

Augustine complains that at the point when he was desperately seeking enlightenment, "There was no time to be had from Ambrose" (T 6.18), and in his early writings he says that it was cruel of the bishop not to help him in his need.[13] His comments on the bishop's concern with worldly adjustments indicate that he thought he and his fellow Christian philosophers considered such a life beneath them: "I thought him [Ambrose] the kind of man made happy in worldly terms by the respect that great people paid him" (T 6.3). This is a reflection of the more sneering tone Augustine took in his early convert days, when he said of church rulers that they were too much in love with power. Even three years after his baptism he could write:

> I hold that neither the men who are swept into administrative tasks by love of earthly glory, nor those who, not yet in office, pine for a public role, have been given the gift, in the babble of their endless meetings and missions, to become death's intimates, as we mean to be—though they could have divinized themselves (deificari) had they retired from the world.[14]

To Augustine, in his haughty early days, Ambrose looked like a demagogue, a trader in dubious miracles, one more interested in adjudicating worldly claims than in paying heed to spiritual distress like Augustine's.

Ambrose no doubt did have an influence on Augustine, but only after the garden scene. Augustine did, finally, get a very full sample of Ambrose's symbolic reading of Scripture—but only during his intensive preparation for baptism, six months after the garden scene—and he did, finally, come to realize the importance of that indoctrination. He first acknowledged its importance five years later.[15] Indeed, Ambrose became increasingly useful to Augustine after he became a bishop himself and had to address many issues of power that he had scorned in his fervent days after baptism. Then, when Augustine's consecration as a bishop was challenged, it became important that he be known as Ambrose's convert. Furthermore, in the fight with the Pelagians over continence, Ambrose was a powerful and moderate alternative to Jerome's views on virginity and sex (O 1.xxxix). But it is anachronistic to read such indebtedness back into Augustine's state of mind before and during the garden scene.

4. The Myth of Suddenness: William James

If what Augustine is telling us is not so much a conversion story as a vocation story, then its use as a pattern of conversion may be misleading. Yet, as I said earlier, it is often taken, along with Paul's story, to establish the very essence of conversion. Both conversions seem abrupt, emotionally charged, with a great lightning bolt dividing the lives of Paul and Augustine into two main parts—and they have been offered as the highest exemplars of conversion. William James had a great deal to do with instilling the notion that conversion is a sudden and once-for-all-time phenomenon. In the two chapters he devoted to conversion in his Gifford Lectures, he wrote, of deep psychological change, that "if the change be a religious one, we call it a conversion, *especially if it be by crisis, or sudden*" (emphasis added).[16] Though James was trying to define the typical experience, he admits that cultural expectation has a great deal to do with how one undergoes (and may invite) mental change. Protestantism, for instance, which throws the whole weight of salvation on a personal and intimate acceptance of grace, leads to a higher rate of conversion in his sense than does Catholicism, which allows one to receive a mediated and socially shared salvation through sacrament and ceremony. But he thinks this is not a matter of mere cultural relativism. Protestantism is closer to the authentic type of conversion because "the adequacy of his [Luther's] view of Christianity to the deeper parts of our human mental structure is shown by its wildfire contagiousness when it was a new and quickening thing."[17] Methodism, too, the religion of revivals, "follows, if not the healthier-minded, yet on the whole the profounder spiritual instinct."[18]

James admits the existence of more gradual, conscious, and self-governing conversion, which he calls the "volitional" change of the "once-born." But he prefers the sudden, semi-conscious, and self-surrendering type of the "twice-born," because it is more radical and more "interesting."[19] He thinks it is more authentic because less consciously controlled: "self surrender has been and always must be regarded as the vital turning point of the religious life."[20] Protestantism lacks some of the aesthetic awareness of Catholicism, "however superior in spiritual profundity it may be to Catholicism"—but that is a small price to pay for profundity.[21] Which should one prefer, better art or "spiritual profundity"?

James was drawing on a burst of new interest in conversion at the end of the nineteenth century. In 1881, Granville Stanley

Hall had delivered at James's own university, Harvard, a series of public lectures on the religiosity of the young. He concluded, from surveys and interviews, that conversion is most common in and around puberty, a thesis he developed in his two-volume work *Adolescence*.[22] He also found that more conversions are gradual than sudden (two thirds to one third). Hall's work was extended and verified in 1897 by Edwin Starbuck, from whom James took the terminology of two types of conversion, those of "volition" and of "self-surrender," while he ignored Starbuck's finding that the average age for conversion of females was 13.8 years and of boys 15.7.[23] Of Starbuck's study, expanded later into the two-volume *Psychology of Religion* (1899), a later scholar wrote: "His work remains today as the most complete and authoritative of its kind."[24]

Starbuck, too, found that most conversions are gradual, not sudden. Though James refers to Starbuck's findings on adolescent conversion, he preferred to collect and study adult accounts of sudden conversion, since they seemed to him more interesting and profound than adolescent stories.[25] That means he is studying the least common type of conversion in the age group where it least occurs. Survey after survey, subjected to analysis after analysis, found the average age of conversion somewhere in the span between ten and nineteen. Paul Emanuel Johnson, conflating the findings of five major studies of conversion, pinpointed the average age at 15.2 years.[26]

Naturally, the experience is not uniform for all teenagers entering into this average—there are variables by class, locale, and education.[27] As James Bissett Pratt put it, conversions come most often to those "brought up in a church or community which taught them to look for it if not to cultivate it."[28] And Johnson says: "The type of conversion is influenced by social expectation. There are styles of conversion, as there are of worship and theology."[29] He thought that adolescent conversions would decline in numbers as "sterner" religion faded in America; but cults, Eastern spirituality, Transcendental Meditation, and New Age concepts continue to provide ample opportunity for teenage conversions. Later studies of converts have confirmed the basic outline of these pioneer investigations.[30]

James's emphasis on suddenness is misleading, since "With most religious people conversion (of the genuine moral sort) is a gradual and almost imperceptible process, with an occasional intensification of emotion now and then during adolescence."[31] James's celebration of crisis-conversions may be unfortunate since it could lead to complacency about the sudden feeling of being saved. One of the most frequent and most studied forms of conversion in our time is the treatment of addiction by "twelve step" programs, where one is warned against the feeling that one heady moment of resolve is an adequate "cure." The emphasis on "steps," on social reinforcement, on mentoring, on "one day at a time," is meant to dispel the illusion that a quick reorientation can be effected. James noticed the conversion experiences of alcoholics—indeed, he quoted an unnamed "medical man" as saying, "The only radical remedy I know for dipsomania is religiomania."[32] But he did not let that distract him from the study of conversions he found "interesting."

Why did James so exclusively direct his attention to sudden

conversion? The reason for that must go farther back than sociological studies at the end of his own century. He grew up in a culture that staked a great deal on the "saving experience" of Puritan culture. He was not raised in a Calvinist family—quite the opposite—and he did not belong to any Congregationalist church. But the individualism, the introversion, the autobiographical urges of the New England region pervaded the culture. The private and temporally precise experience of "being saved" was the condition of membership in Congregationalist churches. This need preyed on the minds of young people, whether they were yearning to join the church, afraid that they could not do so, or determined to defy expectation.

Each person had to meet the Spirit alone, and then give a convincing account of this transforming moment to the examiners of the church. The specific time and place of the rescue were important—as they were in Augustine's garden experience. Joseph Addison, in *The Spectator*, mocked this obsession with the timetable of a Calvinist's conversion, asking a character in one of his essays "what was the occasion of his conversion, upon what day of the month and hour of the day it happened."[33] What Edmund Morgan calls the "demonstration of saving grace" became an art form as well as a personal rite of passage in seventeenth-century Massachusetts.[34] It was something no one else could do for the individual. Even those born into God-fearing families were not presumed to be saved, and therefore qualified to join the church's "visible saints," until the conversion had been privately experienced and publicly aired. It was considered a backsliding, a tainting of the church, when later "halfway covenants" let children of the saved take communion without undergoing their own saving moment.[35]

These conversions would seem to come as close as anyone could wish to the pure model James presents. They are highly conscious, tested by the one undergoing the experience and by those best qualified to judge its nature and effects. Many of them were keyed, like Augustine's conversion, to the impact of a single verse from Scripture.[36] If anything could heal the sick soul and give permanent comfort, it should be this. But the diaries of the time show that the sudden stroke was not as efficacious as the theology shaping it would suggest. Even that paragon of Calvinist awakening, Jonathan Edwards, could never be sure his conversion "took." After he became a pastor in the church, he could still write:

> It seems to me that, whether I am now converted or not, I am so settled in the state that I am in, that I shall go on in it all my life. But, however settled I may be, yet I will continue to pray to God not to suffer me to be deceived about it, not to sleep in an unsafe condition, and ever and anon will call all into question and try myself, using his helps, some of the old divines, that God may have opportunities to answer my prayers, and the spirit of God to show me my error if I am in one.[37]

Edwards was not alone in his uneasiness. The diaries of the converted "saints" in his era show distress and fear that the conversion was not genuine or lasting. Social and personal failings reflected and reinforced each other. As "Jeremiad" sermons said that the community remained sinful, the individuals making it up found their private distress increasing.

Drawing on her extensive use of the letters and diaries of the saints, Patricia Caldwell concluded "that the failure of New England, of state and country alike, to meet the spiritual expectations of the individual who is trying to articulate his experiences, devolves back upon that person and presses him into a doubtful limbo of semiconversion or even nonconversion."[38] The stakes placed on conversion were so high that they induced the very anxieties conversion was meant to dispel. This record makes it seem that James was too sunny-minded himself on the efficacy and permanence of sudden conversions. Conversion was a process, even for those who felt that they *must* be changed suddenly. Edwards deplored the way fervent mass conversions during the Awakening led to relapse. All things considered, it seems that James underestimated what the great Quaker Anthony Benezet called "the inward gradual work of grace."[39]

5. The Myth of Suddenness: Paul

Of course, James could always validate his view of conversion by invoking the least questioned examples of sudden change—the voice that came to Paul on the road to Damascus and the voice that came to Augustine in the garden of Milan. These conversion narratives have some similarities. Both were not only sudden, but were triggered by the intrusion of an external authority. Each involves not a vision but an audition. A voice from heaven asks Paul, "Why do you persecute me?" Another voice, which Augustine takes to be intended for him by God (*divinitus*), says, "Lift! Look!" Former conduct is implicitly condemned—Paul's actions against Christians, Augustine's sexual indulgence. A crisis is passed, leading to the resolution of inner turmoil. On the literal level, there is much to be compared. But how far is a literal reading trustworthy?

It is significant that Paul himself, in all his extensive writings, never tells the story of his experience on the road to Damascus. He tells of other mystical revelations (II Corinthians 12.2–4). He says that Jesus appeared to him (I Corinthians 9.1, 15.8), and that he received his teachings direct from him (Galatians 1.12). But he connects none of his own visions to a conversion experience in general, or to the Damascus road in particular. That story is told only by Luke, in the Acts of the Apostles, where the story is told three different times, a little bit differently each time (9.1–19, 22.1–21, 26.15–18)—which suggests that literal reporting is not the main concern. The important thing for consideration here is that none of Luke's three versions of his tale matches anything Paul says of his mystical experiences. He says later that he saw Jesus, but he does not see anyone in the Damascus event, which involves not a vision but a photism (bright light) and an audition (disembodied voice). Nor does a conversion take place on the spot. Saul is told that he should go to the city and await further enlightenment. It is only after Ananias heals his blindness that

Saul is baptized. This seems to be shorthand for a gradual teaching and healing process that takes place after the photism.

Sending Paul to a city resembles the messages sent to prophets in the Scripture, who are given a mission and a message to deliver. Though Saul is told to receive a teaching rather than to deliver a message, the literary genre that Luke is using to create a double ministry—one for Peter, with direct experience of Jesus, and one for Paul, with indirect experience— seems to draw on vocation stories, not conversion ones. Alan Segal argues that Luke is using the genre of prophetic commissionings as his model in Acts—the Damascus story is especially close to that of Ezekiel's calling.[40] After being stunned by a vision of God's glory (Hebrew *kavod*), Ezekiel says:

When I saw that, I threw myself on my face, and heard a voice speaking to me: Man, he said, stand up and let me talk with you. As he spoke a spirit came into me and stood me on my feet, and I listened to him speaking. He said to me, Man, I am sending you to the Israelites, a nation of rebels who have rebelled against me. Past generations of them have been in revolt against me to this very day, and this generation to which I am sending you is stubborn and obstinate. When you say to them, These are the words of the Lord God, they will know that they have a prophet among them, whether they listen or whether they refuse to listen, because they are rebels. But you, man, must not be afraid of them or of what they say, though they are rebels against you and renegades, and you find yourself sitting on scorpions. There is nothing to fear in what they say, and nothing in their looks to terrify you, rebels though they are. You must speak my words to them, whether they listen or whether they refuse to listen, rebels that they are. But you, man, must listen to what I say and not be rebellious like them (Ezekiel 1.28–2.8, NEB).

At this, a hand appears with a scroll in it, and Ezekiel is told to eat the scroll—acquiring the knowledge he needs for his mission (which is given to Paul by Ananias).

That Segal is not just making a wild guess is confirmed by Luke's third telling of the Damascus tale. In the first two, the voice says simply, "I am Jesus, whom you persecute. Rise up and enter the city and you will be told what you must do" (Acts 9.6). But in the third account, a long speech is recorded, and it is clearly a vocation statement, the call to a mission:

Saul, Saul, why do your persecute me? It is hard only on you to kick back when prodded. . . . I am Jesus, whom you persecute. But rise up and stand firm on your feet. This is why I have appeared to you, to single you out as my worker, as a witness to what you have seen of me and what further things I shall reveal to you, as I rescue you from this people and from the nations to which I am sending you, that you may open their eyes and convert *(epistrepsai)* them from darkness to light, from Satan's thrall to God, so they may, by faith in me, gain forgiveness of sins and a share with the sanctified (Acts 26.15–18).

Luke makes clear here his theological purpose in telling the Damascus story. He intertwines in Acts the missions of Peter and of Paul, one to the Jews, the other to the Gentiles. And since Peter knew Jesus and was directly called by him from his fishing boat, it is important to emphasize that Paul, too, was called, however indirectly. Luke presents the roles of Peter and Paul as complementary, and plays down the conflict between them that Paul is frank about (Galatians 2.11–14). Luke is the author who used Hebrew poetry to create the great canticles of his nativity narrative (Luke 1.46–55, 1.68–79). He has used similar artistry in drawing on the Hebrew tradition of prophetic callings to shape his theological reflection on the meaning of Paul's mission. It compresses into symbolic form what was a more gradual process, made with the help of Ananias, that took Paul from being a Pharisee to being a Christian.

It is important, for Luke's purpose, that all three versions of the Damascus experience begin with the question "Why do you persecute me?" Paul's former persecution is the recommendation he himself uses to show the authority of a gospel *even he* has come to receive. That is how Paul uses his earlier life as a teaching credential (Galatians 1.13). In the same way, Augustine uses the fact that he was not only a heretic but a sinner to show that grace can redeem *even him*. This is typical of the evangelical use of conversion stories (a tactic Augustine justifies in his citation of celebrity converts like Victorinus and Sergius Paul). It is most reasonable to conclude that the Damascus story is Luke's theological construct to give the inner meaning of Paul's ministry its supernatural credentials.

We should also note that the recruiting of other apostles came from a vocation call that only gradually led to conversion in their beliefs: "Come with me, and *I shall make you fishers of men*" (Mark 1.17). The "conversion" of the disciples, the revelation of the meaning of Jesus, was gradual, and was not completed even by Christ's passion and resurrection—since they were told that the full meaning of these would be revealed to them only by the Paraclete, sent after Christ's ascension (John 15.26, 16.7–9). Even if we take the Damascus event as literally true, therefore, Paul would be the exception among apostles in undergoing a sudden conversion, as Pratt noticed.[41] But there are many reasons for not reading Luke literally. Paul himself does not use conversion language *(metanoein, epistrephesthai)* of his response to God, but mission and vocation language *(klētos, apostolos)*.[42] The Luke story is misleading if it is used to say something not only about sudden conversions but about conversion itself. It is mainly a tale of vocation, not of conversion.

6. The Myth of Suddenness: Augustine

Since Augustine tells us he already accepted the doctrines of the church, the only "conversion" in the garden scene is the embrace of celibacy. But why did he think that was a precondition of baptism? The answer to that question is enough to throw doubt on the suddenness of his conversion. He was being pulled toward celibacy and pushed toward it. The pull came from the fact that he was not simply accepting Christianity but aspiring to be a Christian philosopher. Ascetic separation from bodily exigency was part of the concept of a philosopher in Late Antiquity. Augustine tells us in Book Eight [17] that he had aspired to this high calling since reading Cicero's *Hortensius*. That book made Augustine first ask for "chastity, but not yet." The view of the body in *Hortensius* appears from Cicero's comment that the soul is manacled to the body the way corpses were strapped, face to face, on the prisoners of Etruscan pirates.[43] Augustine's low opinion of Ambrose came from the fact that he was too involved in earthly concerns. Augustine and his fellows meant to "divinize" themselves in lofty ascetical contemplation. Their thought was to be too esoteric for general communication. As he wrote from Cassiciacum to another of his circle:

> I think we make enough concessions to our time if some pure stream of Plotinus is channeled through dark and thorny tangles to refresh a few, rather than loosed indiscriminately in the open, where its purity cannot be preserved from the random trampling of cattle.[44]

The distance of this man from the Augustine we know from his later works can be seen in the fact that he dedicates *Happiness in This Life* to Mallius Theodore because he thinks true happiness is not only available on earth *but that Theodore has achieved it*. We can imagine the derision with which Augustine the bishop would treat such a claim.

The vocation to which Augustine felt called used celibacy only as a means—as one of the disciplines to free the mind for philosophical adventures. Augustine shows his bent at Cassiciacum in the *Dialogue with Myself* (line 20) where it is the intellectual life that concerns him.

> *Reason:* I ask you now why you are so concerned that those you love should remain alive, whether with you or away from you?
>
> *Self:* That we may by joint effort explore our own souls and God, so that any who happens first on some knowledge can the more readily share it with the others.
>
> *Reason:* What if they are not interested in such exploration?
>
> *Self:* I shall make them interested.
>
> *Reason:* But what if you fail—what if they think they have sufficient knowledge, or that more is not discoverable, or that other things are more interesting or pleasing?
>
> *Self:* I shall deal with them, and they with me, as best we can.
>
> *Reason:* But what if their presence interferes with your own explorations? If they don't change their ways, won't you take steps, or try to, to be rid of them and their ways?
>
> *Self:* Yes, that's right.
>
> *Reason:* So neither their life in general nor their life with you is desired for its own sake, but only insofar as it helps you in your quest for wisdom?
>
> *Self:* That's it.

If Augustine was being pulled to celibacy by his high intellectual yearnings, he was also being pushed there by his misgivings about marriage. What does he mean by being "forced to put up with unwanted aspects of married life, once bound to it" [2]? If he could not even bear a friend near him who was not dedicated to the intellectual life, is he expressing a fear that any wife would not join his spiritual quest? Of course, he lived with the mother of his child, and loved her deeply, though there is no indication that she had intellectual interests, or was even literate. But that was before he had made his decision to live the pure life of contemplation. The very labored and circuitous way he refers to his problem with marriage indicates that he is being delicate about a more touchy subject—chastity in marriage.

Augustine, like many Christians and some non-Christians, took the view that concupiscence in marriage was sinful. Admittedly, one was allowed to indulge in sex for procreation, though even that should be done in a decorous way, without losing self-control (T 6.22). But where procreation was not possible, sex in marriage was a sin, though a venial one, for the one demanding the act, though not sinful for the one acceding to the demand (out of what Paul called the marriage "debt"— I Corinthians 7.3).[45] Augustine knew himself well enough to recognize that he would not find it easy to be as close to a woman as he was to his son's mother and abstain from sex on all occasions when procreation was not desired and possible. Even if this was only a venial sin in itself, inordinate repetition of the demand could become a more serious matter.[46] Besides, repeated sinfulness and indulgence of the flesh would clash too painfully with the pure aspirations he was entertaining for himself and his intellectual soul mates. Marriage would make a mockery of those ideals. If he could not be "chaste in marriage," it were better to forgo marriage entirely. It was a matter of all or nothing. His attitude at the time of his conversion is plainly stated in the *Dialogue with Myself* (17), When asked by Reason if a beautiful and virtuous wife would appeal to him, Augustine answers:

> Portray her as you will, endow her with every good, yet have I made up my mind that nothing is more to be shunned than union with woman. I know nothing that so topples a man from the defense of his own soul's battlements than female attractions and the fleshly couplings that are the condition of having a wife. If a philosopher is allowed to beget children—a point I am not sure of—then he who has sex only for that purpose gets my admiration but not my imitation. The risk is greater than the chance of success. I have therefore laid this command on myself, rightly and usefully I believe, to protect the freedom of my soul by giving up any concern or quest or contract with a wife.

That passage does not necessarily conflict with the story of the garden, though its tone is certainly different. In the garden, grace breaks the impasse. In the dialogue, Augustine has laid a command on himself, to secure his own freedom. Throughout this section of the dialogue (17), Augustine is being asked about his progress—which is a matter of process, not of an abrupt break or sudden gift.

> *Reason:* I was not asking about what command you gave yourself, but whether you were still struggling with it. Or have you won a clear factor over lust? The subject is still the soundness of your eyes [desire].

Self: Well I am surely not seeking such things any more, nor even longing for them, and when I remember them it is with horror and contempt. What more can you call for? I am making daily progress, since the more I hope to see the beauty I burn for, the more my love and resolve focus on it.

This is a description of gradual conversion ("I am making daily progress"), and of natural motivation (hope strengthens resolve). That the changes being discussed are still in process becomes apparent on the next day (25), when Reason recalls the assurance with which Augustine said that he no longer desired the sex act, but abominated it.

Reason: Last night, surely, as we lay awake pondering between us what had been said, you became aware, for all your confidence to the contrary, how much you were still incited by the bitter sweetness of tempting images, admittedly less powerful than before, yet stronger than you had presumed. It was as if your most intimate Healer were impressing on you both how far you had advanced under his treatment and how far you had to go toward healing.

Self: No more I beg, no more! Why torture me? Why probe me so sharp and deep? I have no strength left for weeping. I can still, even now, keep no promise, make no boast, so do not question me further on this.

Is this the same man who said, at the end of his garden experience, that he was flooded with assurance **[29]**? The dialogue, written at the time, expresses a state of mind far different from the one described eleven years later in *The Testimony*.

7. *The Garden*

Just as the Damascus story is not told by Paul but only later by Luke, so the garden story is not told by Augustine in any of the discussions of his conversion written at the time, but only later in *The Testimony*. That has been enough to raise doubts about its literal truth. A long line of scholars denied the garden story's veracity—Boissier (1888), Harnack (1888), Loofs (1897), Gourdon (1900), Becker (1908), Thimme (1908), Alfaric (1918).[47] But it was not till 1950, when Pierre Courcelle published his assault on the literal reading of Book Eight (among other things), that the debate became widespread and impassioned.[48] O'Donnell says that Courcelle's book "worked a Copernican revolution in Augustine scholarship" (O 1.xxi). He thinks that the emotional resistance to Courcelle's book resembled the previous century's struggle over "higher criticism" of the Bible: "The controversy replicated the earlier battles occasioned by application of scholarly instruments and criteria to biblical texts: literal narrative seemed threatened, and with literal narrative faith itself seemed threatened" (O 1.xxv).

The doubters of the garden story so far cited all work from the contrast between the writings at Cassiciacum and *The Testimony*. But some have been troubled, more generally, by the artificial presentation of the tale, the pat way conversion narratives surge up opportunely and converge on the dramatic climax to Book Eight. Even the highly wrought rhetorical presentation makes some uneasy about the sincerity of the account. Book Eight does not give us a spontaneous account, but a calculated one. Augustine relishes his storytelling gifts—the heightened alliteration, for instance: *volvens et versans me in vinculo* (churning and chafing in my chains). Or the epigrammatic paradoxes: "crazed to be sane . . . dying to be alive." Or the patterns of antithesis: "aware of how bad things were with me, unaware of how good . . ." But if rhetoric of itself precludes truthfulness, then we had better give up on Augustine entirely. He cannot speak at all without using his inmost language, which is rhetoric.

The idea that calculation cannot go with sincerity is naive. Bach's religious music is not insincere because of his immense technical cleverness. Nor is Fra Angelico lacking in piety because he learned Florentine perspective and sophisticated color harmonies. Augustine, in the same way, is a master of words because he sees in their paradoxes the mysteries of the Word. He could describe the soul's interior only through convolutions of language he had mastered as a tool for knowledge, not a mere exercise in ornament. The rhetorical presentation of his own turmoil is no different from his highly rhetorical presentation of the life and suffering of Jesus. He is entirely serious and sincere in both.

Of course, everyone admits that some points in Augustine's treatment of the garden scene are a matter of imagery, not of reportage—the way lusts pluck at his garment, for instance, or attack him from the back; or the way God wields over him a "double whip." No one could think those things were actually seen or suffered in a literal sense. Even more striking is the "revelation" of Self-Control as a female beckoning him to cross over into the company of the pure. Such personification as a way of representing a moral problem was traditional—like the appearance of the Laws to Socrates, asking if he will disobey them by escaping the verdict of his fellow citizens.[49]

Well, what about the fig tree? Was that real or figurative? Why mention it at all if it were real? This was not a moment to digress into dendrology. What relevance can the species of tree have to Augustine's inner state? Courcelle argued, convincingly, that the fig tree was charged with such scriptural symbolism in sermons and Bible commentary, that Augustine must have that tradition in mind when he refers to the fig tree. In that case, *which* scriptural reference was foremost in his mind—the fig tree under which Jesus saw the disciple Nathaniel (John 1.47–48), or the blasted fig tree of the parable (Matthew 21.19–21), or the fig tree from which Adam and Eve took leaves to cover their nakedness (Genesis 2.7)? Courcelle thinks it is the first of these.[50] O'Donnell says that it is all three (O 3.57–58).

One could go along easily with the idea that Self-Control was figurative, as well as the nagging lusts, and the "double whip," and even the fig tree. But Courcelle destroyed the last vestige of literalism when he said that even the voice telling Augustine *Tolle! Lege!*, even the reading of a crucial Pauline verse, were also figurative. He said that the voice was internal, and the reading was a summary of longer delvings into Paul's work. He found support for this in a textual variant. Instead of saying that the voice came from *vicina domo* (a nearby house), one manuscript said that it came from *divina domo* (God's house).[51] But the computer indexing of Augustine's words now establishes that *domus divina* was not a locution Augustine used, with one possible and partial late exception—his preferred form for God's house was *domus Dei* (O 3.59–61).

Besides, if the voice were coming directly from God, why would Augustine not only take the singsong as being chanted by a child, but search his mind to decide whether this was a chant connected with any childhood game he knew? Augustine treats this voice in a way different entirely from the way he responds to his own image of Self-Control. He did not ask himself whether that virtue normally had her arms full of temperate people. He says that Self-Control addressed him in "some such words" as the ones used, not in the direct but puzzling quotation *Tolle! Lege!* Unless that quote were exact, Augustine could not have asked himself to make sense of it. The whole presentation of the child's voice is meant to emphasize its literal reality. If there was no such literal reality, then Augustine has been at some pains to deceive us. If we are not to call Augustine a liar, then, we must conclude, as unambiguously as Courcelle concludes the opposite, that the voice was real.

But that does not mean that Courcelle's approach is fundamentally wrong. The point is not whether the voice occurred, but what Augustine made of its occurrence, both at the time and in writing *The Testimony*. After all, other events actually occurred, but were used retrospectively to make theological points in Augustine's program for *The Testimony*. The pear theft's meaning is elaborated far beyond the literal facts involved, presuming (as I do) that there were some literal facts at the base of the elaborations. The same is true for his father's comment in the public baths, for the death of Augustine's friend, and for the garden experience with Monnica. All are the subject of later reflection on their ultimate meaning for Augustine, yet all depart in some way from what can be accepted as a real event.

I would go further, and say that they all have meanings that are linked with the overall structure of *The Testimony*, and therefore with the book of Genesis. The entire *Testimony* moves toward the probing of the mysteries of God to be found in the opening book of the Bible. Augustine's *Testimony* is an act of purification from sin, of the kind priests invoke as they prepare to read Scripture in public. It is, then, a prayer to be made worthy, a petition for entry into the sacred revelation. In this light, Augustine is approaching Genesis by a process that attunes him to it, makes him see its patterns in his own life, revealing the relevance of what he has undergone to what he is proposing. It is a case of ontogeny forecasting phylogeny. Each of the events in the book that is given profound theological reflection has a relationship to the Genesis mysteries.

1. *The public baths.* The first vivid event reported in *The Testimony* comes near the beginning of Book Two—the observation

of Augustine's sexual maturity by his father (T 2.6). Up to this point, Augustine's memories were vague or generic—of childhood stealing, delinquency from school, resistance to learning Greek. The most specific thing mentioned in Book One was an illness that made him cry for baptism; but this event too is described vaguely—the disease is not named, nor are his mother's comments directly quoted. The scene in the public baths is far more specific—it even tells us what was going through his father's mind (that now he could have grandchildren).

Why is this vivid scene included in the book? Various psychosexual explanations have been resorted to; but the norms of inclusion in this book are primarily theological. Considering how much is omitted—all about his siblings, for instance, or his life under Romanian's patronage in Thagaste—one must ask why this, of all things, is reported. Those who think Augustine is obsessed with sex have answers for this—too many answers, in fact.[52] Few concentrate on what is the most surprising and revealing word in the passage, *indutum*. Augustine says that he was nude but was "clothed in unstable young manhood." "Unstable" *(inquietum)* because man is fallen, no longer secure in the garden of Eden—our heart, Augustine memorably says, is unstable *(inquietum)* until stabilized in God (T 1.1).[53] He is clothed, as the naked Adam was "clothed," in the shame of a damaged humanity—which Adam tried to cover with fig leaves.

The encounter with his father in the public baths looks forward to Book Eight's garden scene, where he moves from the fig tree to Paul's admonition to "be clothed *(induite)* in Christ."

That is what happens at baptism. The baptizands, after undergoing a *scrutatio*—an inspection of the body, like (but how unlike) his father's gaze—went naked into the water, to come out on the other side and be clothed in Christ, wearing white robes of regained innocence.

2. *The pear theft.* Critics of Augustine, typified by Nietzsche, have mocked the inflation of what would later be called "a second-rate burglary" in the long agonizings of Book Two. The first sin reported in Augustine's time of young manhood is not sexual, but a gratuitous act, not motivated by desire for the stolen fruits. Because the act seems at first undriven by passion, this sin comes close to what Augustine considered the primary characteristic of Adam's sin—that it took place without the distortions of passion resulting from that act. It was sin in an unfallen state, a cold act of disobedience [22]. Augustine's sin-for-its-own-sake approximates the passionless original sin.

Of course, after long psychological rumination, Augustine concludes that his sin was not really motiveless—he would not have done it alone, so his motive was solidarity with his fellow delinquents (T 2.17). That, too, brings the sin close to Adam's, since Augustine argued that Adam was not swayed, as Eve was, by the Devil's spurious promises—Adam knew they were false. Then whey did he sin? He did it for the comradely compulsion *(socialis necessitudo)* of solidarity with Eve.[54] There can be no doubt that Augustine wants this scene to be read as referring back to the sin of Adam. He says that the young felons took away huge loads *(onera ingentia,* T 2.9) of pears, and the hell-raising would hardly have made its mark if only one tree were stripped—yet Augustine refers to a symbolic single tree, to underline its relationship with the tree in Eden. A passionless sin is what is at issue when Augustine takes up the heritage of original sin by, in effect, repeating its commission. This puts the pear scene in alignment, as well, with the scene in the baths that preceded it in Book Two. The shame-in-nudity at the baths showed the potential of sin inherited from Adam. The pear theft shows that potential becoming a reality.[55]

3. *The friend's death.* A second occasion for agonizing, and for Nietzsche's mockery of Augustine's self-reference, is the emotional reaction to his friend's death described in such detail at *The Testimony* 4.7–12. It is the impurity of his motives for grief that is emphasized there, the selfishness at his own loss, the anger that he could not bring the friend to renounce the baptism he had undergone. He uses a citation from Psalm 41.6 to reveal his anger at not being able to deprive his friend of the gift God had given him. The psalm says: *Quare tristis es, anima mea, et quare conturbas me?* (Why, in your anguish, are you, my soul, whirling me about?) God asks of Cain, angry at Abel's acceptance by God: *Quare tristis factus es, et quare concidit facies tuus?* (Why, in your anguish, is your face twisted about?) Once again, Genesis is echoed in Augustine's own life.

4. *The garden scene with Monnica.* The garden, that recurring scriptural image, once again plays a key role in the scene of Augustine's shared mystical silence with his mother (T 9.25).

After his baptism, Augustine is clothed in Christ, saved from the consequences of original sin, so far as that is possible in one's lifetime, and the harmony of the garden of Eden (before original sin ruined it) is partly experienced, or almost experienced, for a moment in this scene of reconciliation not so much between Monnica and Augustine, as between humankind and its Creator.

5. *The garden scene in Book Eight.* All of the other references to Genesis themes in Augustine's life come to a climax in his garden "conversion." He reverses the progress of Adam by moving from the fig tree of sinful shame to the innocence regained by being clothed in Christ. But there is a further resonance here as well. Gardens are symbolically charged places in Scripture, and Augustine's agony in the garden is bound to suggest the greatest agony in a garden, that of Jesus himself. What some consider the emotionally overwrought descriptions of Augustine's suffering are not more extreme than the words used of Jesus in the gospels. He is sorrowful unto death, so worked upon that he sweats blood, so afflicted that he asks that the cup of suffering pass him by—though he finally surrenders his will to the will of another, using the very words of the greatest Christian prayer, "Thy will be done" *(Fiat voluntas tua).*

Augustine, too, is tortured unto death—"dying to be alive" **[19]**. He too is asked to undergo a suffering sent by God, who is "wielding the double whip" over him **[25]**. Though he does not sweat blood, he is drenched "in great sheets of showering

tears" [28]. To stress the connections between these two ago-
nies in the garden, Augustine first enters the garden with
Alypius, then leaves him behind, silent and excluded from the
agony, before rejoining him to go forth to Monnica. In the
same way, Jesus enters the garden with three of his closest disciples, leaves them behind to fall asleep in their ignorance of
what he is undergoing, then rejoins them to go forth to his
task. The New Testament garden is here joined with that of
Genesis, since clothing oneself in Christ can only happen because God suffered with man by becoming incarnate, clothing
himself in flesh. The anguish of Adam has to be undone by the
agony of Jesus. Augustine, as the heir of that great triumph,
moves backward from sin to regain innocence through the
redemptive suffering of Christ. He goes from being clothed
(indutus) in nakedness to the passage of Paul that says "Be
clothed." (This is not a matter of Augustine "presuming" to
link his suffering with Christ's, but of Christ coming down to
share all the miseries of humankind, while remedying them.)
The rich resonances of the garden scene contain more of Christ
than of Adam. That is the theological meaning of the decision
to be baptized.

The myths of conversion in Book Eight are, therefore, all
myths elaborated by Augustine himself. They reveal what was
going on "behind the scenes," as it were, things he was not
aware of at the time—the power of grace in Monnica's prayer
and Ambrose's example, the action of God in his own efforts
toward chastity. This is a kind of palinode to the earlier writings, which relied too much (Augustine has come to believe) on

natural causes and personal effort, on Mallius Theodore and "Platonic books." The conversion myths are devised to show that God directed the sequence by which Augustine was "making daily progress."

Is the garden scene not true, then? Only if we assume, as too many do, that Augustine is writing an autobiography. He is not. The whole work, and not just the final books, is a theological work, a preparation for the reading of Scripture, for an entry into God's mysteries which God must himself make possible. The God of Genesis is not a text in the past, but an unrecognized constant in Augustine's life, "deeper in me than I am in me" (*intimior intimo meo*, T 3.11). The garden scene is based on a real event, as were the scenes in the public baths, in the pear orchard, at his friend's deathbed, or with Monnica in Ostia. But they all fit into a larger testimony that celebrates the word of God more than the life of Augustine.

Notes to Introduction

1. For Monnica as the proper (African) spelling of her name, see W.H.C. Frend, *The Donatist Church* (Oxford University Press, 1951), p. 250.
2. Rebecca West, *St. Augustine* (D. Appleton & Co., 1933), pp. 26–27.
3. For Augustine's early rejection of post–New Testament miracles, see *Order in Creation* 2.7.7, on people "daunted by hollow claims of the miracles," and *The True Religion* 25.47, "Miracles are not permitted to stretch into the present, or the soul would always be looking for sensations, and the human race would grow jaded with their continual occurrence."
4. Augustine, *Order in the Universe* 1.11.
5. Augustine, *Happiness in This Life* 2.10, 2.16.
6. *Order in the Universe* 2.45.
7. Ibid. 2.10.
8. Pierre Courcelle, *Recherches sur les Confessions de saint Augustin* (Boccard, Editeur, 1950), pp. 28–32.
9. *Happiness in This Life* 1.45.
10. Given the importance of both figures, any genuine correspondence between Augustine and Ambrose would instantly have been copied and widely disseminated. It is striking that not even forged letters have ever surfaced.
11. For Augustine's changed views of Theodore, see his *Reconsiderations* on *Happiness in This Life:* "Though the man I dedicated this book to was a scholar and a Christian, I gave him more credit than he deserved" (O 2.419–20).
12. *Happiness in This Life* 1.4–5.
13. Augustine, *Dialogue with Myself* 2.26.
14. Epistle 10.2.
15. Augustine, *The Uses of Belief* 8.20.
16. William James, *The Variety of Religious Experience*, in *Writings 1902–1910* (The Library of America, 1987), p. 183.
17. Ibid., p. 226.
18. Ibid., p. 211.
19. Ibid., p. 193.
20. Ibid., p. 196.

21. Ibid., p. 213.
22. G. Stanley Hall, *Adolescence* (D. Appleton & Co., 1904).
23. Edwin D. Starbuck, "A Study of Conversion," *American Journal of Psychology*, January 1897, p. 80.
24. Elmer T. Clark, *The Psychology of Religious Awakening* (Macmillan, 1929), p. 19. Starbuck's book is *The Psychology of Religion* (Charles Scribner's Sons, 1899).
25. James, op. cit., pp. 185–86.
26. Paul Emanuel Johnson, *Psychology of Religion* (Abingdon-Cokesbury Press, 1920, 1959), pp. 100–101: "The more radical awakenings of crisis tend to occur about the age of seventeen—which coincides with earlier reports of Starbuck and Hall. But when religion develops as a gradual process, the awakening comes as early as twelve years. If the process is interrupted or resisted at this age, it is then deferred about five years and requires an emotional crisis to overcome obstruction." Twelve was the average age Elmer T. Clark set for conversion (op. cit., p. 17).
27. There are elaborate tables breaking down this information in Clark, op. cit.
28. James Bissett Pratt, *The Religious Consciousness* (Macmillan, 1920), p. 153.
29. Johnson, op. cit., p. 99.
30. See, for instance, Bernard Spilka, Ralph W. Hood, Jr., and Richard L. Gorsuch, *The Psychology of Religion: An Empirical Approach* (Prentice-Hall, 1985), pp. 199–224.
31. Pratt, op cit., p. 153.
32. James, op. cit., p. 246.
33. Joseph Addison, *The Spectator* (Oxford University Press, 1965), vol. 4, p. 252.
34. Edmund Morgan, *Visible Saints: The History of a Puritan Idea* (New York University Press, 1963), p. 90.
35. Ibid., pp. 10–38.
36. Patricia Caldwell, *The Puritan Conversion Narrative* (Cambridge University Press, 1983), pp. 169–72.
37. Edwards diary quoted in George M. Marsden, *Jonathan Edwards: A Life* (Yale University Press, 2003), p. 105.
38. Caldwell, op. cit.

39. George S. Brookes, *Friend Anthony Benezet* (University of Pennsylvania Press, 1937), p. 308.
40. Alan F. Segal, *Paul the Convert: The Apostolate and Apostasy of Saul the Pharisee* (Yale University Press, 1990), pp. 8–11.
41. Pratt, op. cit., p. 155.
42. Segal, op. cit., p. 19.
43. Albert Grilli, *Ciceronis Hortensius* (Istituto editoriale cisalpina, 1962), p. 52.
44. Epistle 1.1.
45. Augustine, *What Is Good in Marriage* 6–7.
46. Ibid. 6.
47. The doubters' works are cited in Charles Boyer, *Christianisme et néo-platonisme dans la formation de Saint Augustin* (Gabriel Duchesne, 1920), pp. 2–6.
48. Courcelle, op. cit.
49. Plato, *Crito* 50–54.
50. Courcelle, op. cit., p. 193.
51. Ibid., pp. 195–96.
52. Psychiatrist Charles Kligerman thinks that Augustine's father found him with an erection (*Journal of the American Psychoanalytic Association* 5, 1957, pp. 469 ff.). Psychiatrists R. Braendle and W. Neidhardt think he found his son masturbating (*Theologische Zeitschrift* 40, 1984, pp. 157 ff.). The claims have nothing to do with the text or with the practices of Roman baths. See further in my *Saint Augustine* (Viking, 1999), pp. xvii–xix.
53. For more on Augustine's statics, see my *Saint Augustine's Childhood* (Viking, 2001), pp. 83–89.
54. Augustine, *City of God* 14.11.
55. For more on the pear theft, see my *Saint Augustine's Sin* (Viking, 2003), pp. 7–19.

PART II

The Testimony:
Book Eight

❦

Notes

L1 *call to mind*] Isaiah 63.7: "I will call to mind the Lord's acts of pity."

L2 *shed over me*] Psalm 85.13: "great is your pity shed over *(super)* me."

L2 *suppled with*] Like the dry bones revivified of Ezekiel 37.1–14.

L3 *Who is your like*] Psalm 34.10: "My very bones ask, Who is your like, Lord."

L3 *You struck*] Psalm 115.17: "You struck off my chains, a praise offering I will sacrifice to you."

L6 *Blessed be God*] II Chronicles 1.12: "Blessed be the God of Israel, who made heaven and earth."

L6 *great his honor*] Psalm 8.2: "how your honor *(nomen)* is to be wondered at forever.

L7 *inner bastion*] Literally, the "fore-heart." The gains God has made with Augustine are being solidified—already he has yielded on the key objection he had, that God was not pure spirit.

L9 *mirror's wavering image*] I Corinthians 13.12: "Now we see in a mirror's wavering image *(aenigma)*." Given ancient mirror technology, one did not see *through* a glass, darkly, as the old translation had it, but *in* a beaten bronze surface, unevenly.

L14 *old ferment*] I Corinthians 5.8: "Let us not use the old ferment in our celebration of the holy day, the ferment of malice and malignity, but use the unfermented bread of sincerity and truth."

L21 *Path should be followed*] O'Donnell prefers the manuscripts that give Life *(vitae)* rather than Path *(viae)*, but that seems pleonastic with *viveret* earlier in the sentence and ignores the way Augustine needs guidance on the Path (at the end of the sentence). John 14.6: "I am the Path."

Searching for Help

1.   Gratefully, my God, may I 'call to mind and testify to your pities shed over me.' My very bones, suppled with infusion of your love, ask: 'Who is your like, Lord?' 'You struck off my chains, a praise-offering I will sacrifice to you.' I shall tell how you struck them off, so all who worship you may say on hearing it: 'Blessed be God, on earth as in heaven, great his honor, and to be wondered at.' With your words fixed in my inner bastion, you also fortified my outer works. I was sure, now, that you lived outside time, though I saw this 'as in a mirror's wavering image.' I no longer questioned the fact that there is one reality that cannot decay, from which are derived all other realities. Now I wanted more to rest in you than to reason about you, for my own life inside time was unstable, and my heart was 'unpurged of its old ferment.' Though drawn to the Path, who is my savior, I shied from its hard traveling.

You then prompted me—and I saw on consideration how wisely—to approach Simplician, who was your good servant in my eyes, glowing with your bounty. Beyond that, I had learned at second hand how true to you he had been from his childhood, and I considered him now, after his living long and deeply mulling the way your Path should be followed, to be a man great in experience and learning—as he proved to be. I

L2 *produce from his store*] Matthew 13.52: "who produces from his store rich things both old and new."

L2 *tread your Path*] Psalm 127.1: "and blessed those who tread your paths."

L5 *some this gift, some that*] I Corinthians 7.7: "but each has his own gift from God, some this gift, some that."

L9 *the orderliness of your house*] Psalm 25.8: "the orderliness *(decus)* of your house I have loved, Lord."

L12 *to be as he was*] I Corinthians 7.7: "I would prefer all men to be as I am."

L15 *unwanted aspects*] Augustine would still have to face the problem of chastity *within marriage* [*comm.*].

L18 *the reign of the heavens*] Matthew 19.12 (Vulgate): "and other have castrated themselves for the heavenly (plural *caelorum*) reign."

L18 *claim it*] Matthew 19.12: "Choose it who can."

L20 *men so empty*] Wisdom 13.1–3:

L22 *was rising . . . was recognizing*] Imperfect tenses used of a process *(transcenderam, inveneram).*

determined to consult him about my seethings, that he might 'produce from his store' a rule for one in my condition to 'tread your Path.'

2. The church, I could see, was filled with people who had 'some this gift, some that.' As for me, the life I had led disgusted me. No longer on fire, as before, with ambition for glory or wealth, I could not bear the slave's grind of getting them. They could not be compared with your sweetness or 'my love for the orderliness of your house.' But woman still held me firmly in her grasp. The apostle, it is true, did not forbid marriage, however much he urged a higher way, earnestly wanting others 'to be as he was.' Yet I in my frailty was opting for the softer course, and apart even from my general lassitude, debilitated as I was by flaccid anxieties, I returned always to one concern: whether I would be forced to put up with unwanted aspects of married life, once bound to it. I have it from the voice of truth that 'There are eunuchs who have castrated themselves for the reign of the heavens.' But he [also] says, 'Claim it who can.'

Mine was no longer the emptiness of 'those men so empty that they see no God, unable to discover in the apparently good the one who is truly good.' From such vanity I was rising, I was recognizing the one to whom all created things give joint testimony, discovering you, the creator of us all; and, along with you, your Word, who is also God, one God with you, and the one 'through whom you created all things.' As for the other category of the irreligious, those who see that there is a God but do not honor him as God and give him their gratitude—

L2 *To be wise*] Job 18.18 (Vulgate): For see, to be wise is to honor God."

L3 *to be known as wise*] Wisdom 7.5: "The wise man would not be known as wise."

L4 *proclaiming their own wisdom*] Romans 1.22: "Those proclaiming their own wisdom were stultified."

L5 *the precious pearl*] Matthew 13.45–46: "discovering one precious pearl, went to sell all his possessions and bought it."

I was slipping into that category until your right hand took and lifted me high to a healthy place, just as you told us: 'To be wise is to honor God.' And: 'Seek not to be known as wise.' And: 'those proclaiming their own wisdom were stultified.' I was 'discovering the precious pearl, to buy which I should have sold all my possessions.' But I held back.

L2 *reception of your bounty*] Simplician baptized Ambrose, when Ambrose was elected bishop and had not even undergone baptism.

L3 *at the time*] This part of *The Testimony* was therefore written after 397, when Ambrose died and Simplician himself succeeded him as bishop of Milan.

L6 *Victorinus*] Caius Marius Victorinus, a rhetorician and St. Jerome's teacher, seems never to have translated "books of the Platonists" [*comm.*].

L9 *sophistries . . . worldly principles*] Colossians 2.8: "Be not misled by philosophy and vain sophistries inspired by human teaching, inspired by worldly principles, not inspired by Christ."

L10 *haunted*] Writings into which truth could be spirited *(insinuari)*.

L12 *a thing hidden*] Matthew 11.28: "because you have hidden these things from the wise and prudent, and revealed them to the insignificant."

First Conversion Story: Victorinus

3. To Simplician, then, I proceeded. In administering the reception of your bounty, he had been a father to Ambrose, who was bishop at the time, and it was as a father that Ambrose loved him. I told him how I had wandered in a labyrinth of falsehoods. When I let him know that I had read certain writings of the Platonists, those translated into Latin by Victorinus— once an orator at Rome, who died (so I had heard) a Christian— he felt cheered at my prospects, since I had not chanced on other philosophers' writings, dense with sophistries and false leads inspired by worldly principles, but on writings haunted in all kinds of ways by God and his Word. Then, the better to prompt me toward Christ's lowliness, 'a thing hidden from the wise but revealed to the insignificant,' he called to mind this very Victorinus, who had been his friend while he was in Rome, and he told me his story—nor will I refrain from repeating what he said, since it deserves the testimony of praise to your bounty.

Here was a man who reached a learned old age, skilled in all the liberal arts, one who had read all the philosophers and could sift their worth, who had taught many of the most distinguished senators, had even earned and accepted the honor of having his statue raised in the Roman forum (a thing citizens

L4 *X*] The manuscript begins the list of foreign gods with a jumble of letters no one has convincingly sorted out (O 3.17–18).

L4 *spawn missbegotten*] Virgil, *Aeneid* 8.690–700:

> Spawn misbegotten of mongrel deities,
> With latrant god Anubis—the gods who chased
> Neptune and Venus, Minerva, off the field.

L5 *latrant*] Anubis is the dog-god who barks.

L7 *their vanquished*] Augustine thinks the old Roman gods foolish enough, but preferable to the foreign gods of conquered peoples, who were preferred to them by a decadent Rome—and by Victorinus!

L9 *but at the end*] This long cyclical sentence stresses three things in connection with Victorinus' old age, which is emphasized in connection with all three—his long study and deep learning in secular culture, his long defense of the evil mysteries from the East, and his break from the learning and the idolatry when he became purified as a child in baptism. The breaking away from the past—the point that Simplician is making as he tells this story to the hesitating Augustine—is reenacted, almost miraculously, in this single virtuoso sentence.

L10 *humbling his neck*] Wisdom 51.34: "Humble your necks under the yoke."

L11 *with your cross*] At baptism the forehead was sealed with a sign of the cross.

L12 *bent the heavens*] Psalm 143.5: "Lord, bend down the heavens to ride on them, touch to smoldering the mountains." Augustine, in his sermon on this psalm, calls the heavens the Lord rides on the apostles who preach the faith, and calls the mountain struck (by lightning) the high pride of men—in other words, the *intellectual* component of conversion, and the *moral* component. Victorinus' case, as explained by the psalm, is that he had already received the truth (from the heavens) but needed the blow of grace to his pride (the mountains). The application to Augustine's case is obvious.

L25 *cedars of Lebanon*] Psalm 18.5: "The Lord levels the cedars of Lebanon."

L28 *rejected by Christ*] Luke 12.9: "Whoever rejects me in the presence of men will be rejected in the presence of God's angels."

of this world so highly prize) because of the great worth of his instruction, yet was also, deep into his years, a cultist of idols, the celebrant of evil rites, with which almost all the nobility had grown giddy—with [X], with a 'spawn misbegotten of mongrel deities, with latrant god Anubis, with the gods who chased Neptune, Venus, and Minerva, off the field,' as Rome bowed to the gods of their vanquished subjects—all this Victorinus, even in his age, had defended with earthshaking eloquence, but at the end he did not blush to become a child of your Christ, an infant at your font, 'humbling his neck under your yoke' and branding his vanquished forehead with your cross.

4.   Lord, O Lord, you who have bent the heavens to ride down on them, who struck to smoldering the mountains, how more subtly did you strike that man's heart? It was his practice, as Simplician told me, to read holy writ, to study other Christian writings constantly and carefully, until he said to Simplician, in the confidence of friendship, making no public statement: You can count me a Christian by now. Simplician answered: I put no trust in that, nor rank you among Christians, till the day I see you in Christ's church. And he taunted back: Are Christians made by walls? So the one man kept claiming to be a Christian, the other making him the same answer, and the first repeated his taunt about walls. Victorinus did not want to lose the respect of his peers, those proud idolaters, from the height of whose Babylonian pride, as from 'cedars of Lebanon not yet leveled by the Lord,' he feared a landslide of contempt. But by longer reading, by panting after truth, he drank in strength. He was now more afraid of being 'rejected by Christ in the presence of holy angels'

L1 *testifying to Christ*] Luke 12.8: "Whoever testifies to me in the presence of men, to him will the son of man testify before God's angels."

L5 *hollow . . . holy*] Repeating the play of sound and thought in *vanitati . . . veritati.*

L12 *raged at the sight*] Psalm 111.10: "The sinner will rage at the sight, grind his teeth and pine away."

than of 'testifying to Christ in the presence of men.' He himself counted it a great crime to blush at accepting the holy rites of your Word's lowliness, when he had not blushed at the evil rites of the devils' haughtiness, himself haughty as he mimicked them, shameless toward hollow things, ashamed of holy things.

But then he said out of the blue, when Simplician was least expecting it: Go we to the church, I would be a Christian. Simplician, barely containing his delight, set off with him. There Victorinus was steeped in the basic mysteries of the faith, and shortly after entered his name for the rebirth of baptism, to Rome's astonishment and the church's rejoicing. The haughty 'raged at the sight, grinding their teeth, pining away.' But your servant now placed all his hope in the Lord God, no longer concerned with hollow things, with the illusions of deceit.

5. So when it came time for him to profess the creed—a thing that was done in Rome by a candidate for your bounty with words exactly formulated, memorized, and delivered from a high place before all the faithful—Simplician used to say that the elders offered him the option of making a secret profession, as they normally did to those who might falter from embarrassment. But he wished to proclaim his rescue before the holy congregation. He had, after all, publicly taught rhetoric, which rescued him from nothing. Why shy before your calm flock, when voicing your Word, if he did not shy from a wild mob of the bemused, when using words of his own? As he climbed to the place for reciting the creed, all those who recognized him— and who did not?—raised the glad outcry: Victorinus! Then the whole rejoicing crowd repeated in low whispers: Victorinus! The

L10 *one returning*] Luke 15.7: "I tell you there will be more joy in heaven over one sinner returning than over ninety-nine, not sinning, who have no need to return" (taking *paenitentia* as a turn against sin).

L12 *shepherd's glad shoulders*] Luke 15.5: "and when he [the shepherd] finds it, he is glad to lift it on his shoulders."

L14 *neighbors of the woman*] Luke 15.9: "and when she [the woman] finds it, calls in her friends and neighbors and says 'Be happy with me.' "

L17 *was dead and is living*] Luke 15.24: "my [prodigal] son was dead and is living, was lost and is found."

L28 *go pallid*] Virgil, *Aeneid* 44.644: "[Dido] goes pallid as her death impends."

sudden shouts were from excitement at seeing him, and the sudden quieting was for concentration on hearing him. He recited the truths of the creed with an evident firmness, and they wished to clasp him to their breast, and the two hands clasping him were their love and their joy.

6. Good our God, what is going on within a man when he is happier to see the rescue of one there was no hope for, snatched from a terrible plight, than of one always hoped for or in no terrible plight? Well, even you, the father of pity, have greater joy 'for one returning than for ninety-nine who never strayed,' and we hear again with joy, no matter how many times it is repeated, of the 'stray sheep being returned on the shepherd's glad shoulders,' or how the small coin is returned to your coffers while 'neighbors of the woman who found it are happy with her.' Even while the mass is being celebrated in your house with joy, there are tears in your house when it is read how that younger son of yours 'was dead and is living, was lost and is found.' It is your joy we feel in us, and that of your angels, made holy by their holy love. For you, always the same, are unvarying in your knowledge of what is varying and never the same.

7. What, I ask again, is going on in a man that makes him happier with loved things found or returned than if he had possessed them always? Other examples [than the scripture texts] confirm this, and life is full of evidence that fairly cries out that this is so. The conquering general prevails, but at the cost of having to fight a battle, and the greater the battle's damage, the greater joy conquest brings. A sea storm throws about those in a boat, and threatens to destroy the boat—all 'go pallid as their

L1 *grow calm*] Luke 8.24: "[Jesus] chid the wind, and the sea storm ended, and all was calm."

L2 *just as hysterical*] The force of repeated *nimis . . . nimis.*

L10 *eat salty things*] An example of Augustine's gift for earthy comparisons [*comm.*].

L13 *delivered . . . delayed*] Repeats the play on *maritus datam . . . sponsus dilatam.*

L16 *was dead*] Luke 15.24: "my [prodigal] son was dead and is living, was lost and is found."

L19 *your . . . you yourself*] Emphatic *tu . . . tibi, tu ipse.*

L19 *those near you*] Referring to angels, by contrast with the lower "our part" in the next clause.

L24 *from the highest*] Matthew 24.31: "and [angels] will gather the saved from all four winds, from the highest of the heavens to the lowest."

death impends.' Then 'sea and sky grow calm,' and people are just as hysterical with joy as they had been with fear. A friend is stricken ill; his pulse portends the worst; all who hope for him are ill in spirit with him. Should he recover, though crippled, his friends are happier at this than they were when he walked with perfect health and vigor. Men even cultivate their pleasures, not taking them as they come, spontaneously and unplanned, but after deprivations arranged on a plan. Pleasure in food and drink is provoked by prearranged hunger or thirst, as when drunkards eat salty things to dry up their mouths, to make the soothing draft more pleasurable. Society arranges that promised brides be not instantly handed over, lest the man, as a husband, should hold lightly the prize delivered, if not forced as a groom to sigh for the prize delayed.

8. It is just as true in vile and detestable joys, in innocent and licit loves, and in this example of one 'who was dead and is living, was lost and is found,' that joy is always greater after greater affliction. Why should this be the case, Lord my God, when your eternal joy is you yourself, and those near you have joy in you, while it is our part to be tossed between loss and gain, between disjoinings and rejoinings? Is this the natural bent of things, and did you ordain it so, you who order all that you created as good, all proper beings in their proper times and places, 'from the highest of the heavens to the lowest of the earth,' from time's beginning to its end, from angel to worm, from first stirring of existence to its completion? Yet you are highest of the high, and I, alas, am lowest of the low, and barely we arrive at you who never depart from us.

L4 *come to you*] Psalm 33.6: "Come to him and be illuminated."

L5 *receive from you*] John 1.12: "To all receiving him, honoring his honor, he gave the power of being God's sons."

L14 *the rich are preferred*] Deuteronomy 1.17: "You will hear the great and the small, nor will you prefer any person whoever."

L15 *you have chosen the powerless*] I Corinthians 1.27–28: "You have chosen the powerless of the world to thwart the powerful, the ignorant of the world to thwart the wise, and the nobodies of the world to be somebodies, making the somebodies of no account."

L17 *chosen the nobodies*] Romans 4.17: "he makes the dead live and summons those who are nobodies to be somebodies."

L20 *least of your apostles*] I Corinthians 15.9: "For I am the least of the apostles."

L22 *[Sergius] Paul*] Acts of the Apostles 13.7–12: The apostle Paul converted the proconsul Paul by confounding a magician in his court. Since this is the first time Acts (at verse 9) mentions the change of Paul's name (from Saul), Augustine takes it that the name was assumed to commemorate the victory of another Paul's conversion. This is another way of playing up this book's concentration on conversion [*comm.*].

L22 *your gentle yoke*] Matthew 11.30: "for my yoke is gentle." This and "warred down" are perfect examples of the way Augustine can weave into one quote both the Bible and Virgil's poetry.

Second Conversion Story: Sergius Paul

9. Come, Lord, shake us and carry us away, be a fire and a sweetness to us, since we would love, would run the race. Some men sunk even deeper than Victorinus was in a pit of blinding darkness, turn back and 'come to you and are illuminated, receiving light.' Those who receive the light 'receive from you the power of being your sons.' But if they are not celebrities, even those who are aware of their conversion are less joyful over it, since individual affection is increased by being shared with others, by a kind of contagion or mutual conflagration. Celebrities reach more people by their good example, and where they go others will follow to their own rescue. They give joy therefore even to those who have preceded them on the way, since the joy is not just for a single person. This is far from saying that 'the rich are preferred in your holy place to the poor, or the highborn to the lowborn'—on the contrary, 'you have chosen the powerless of the world to confound the powerful, chosen the unknown and disregarded, and chosen the nobodies to be somebodies, making the somebodies of no account.' Nonetheless, the very man through whom you voiced these words, 'the least of your apostles,' was glad to be no longer Saul but Paul because of a great victory—when, by his campaigning, the proconsul [Sergius] Paul 'submitted to your gentle yoke, all his

L1 *pride warred down*] Virgil, *Aeneid* 6.863: "To spare the yielding but war down the proud."

L1 *officer of the great King*] Augustine called the clergy warriors of God and the laity his officers *(proviniciales),* as at *The Asssignment of Monks* 15.27: "you are officers of the great King."

L10 *bound the strong*] Matthew 12.29: "How is one to enter a strong man's home and seize his vessels without first binding the strong man?"

L11 *a thing useful*] II Timothy 2.21: "Whoever shall cleanse himself of these [ignoble uses] will be a vessel consecrated for honorable service, made useful for all the Lord's good work."

pride warred down,' and became 'an officer of the great King.'
Satan is more baffled when he loses one in his thrall through
whom many others were in his thrall. He holds the proud by
their claim to high title and he holds others by their reverence
for that title. That is why Victorinus' submission was so prized—
not only of his heart, which the Devil had claimed as a vessel
not to be wrested from him, but of his tongue, which the Devil
had used as a sharp great spear for destroying many. Your children, Lord, had reason for their greater celebration when our
King 'bound the strong man and seized his vessels,' to clean
them for your honor's service, as 'a thing useful for all the
Lord's good work.'

L3 *later*] Augustine is not, then, telling us of one conversation with Simplician but of a series, in which Simplician leads him on by adding further information about Victorinus, once he has seen the effect of his earlier comments.

L7 *the tongues of wordless*] Wisdom 10.21: "You make the tongues of wordless babes eloquent."

L8 *more relieved than reluctant*] To reproduce the play on *fortior . . . felicior.*

L11 *static will*] Literally, "iron will." But our idiom makes "iron" mean strong when it is applied to the will, where inert is the meaning intended. So "static" must serve both for the will and for the "iron imposition" (Julian's decree) paired with it.

L18 *give you free worship*] Job 1.9 (Vulgate): "Does not Job give the Lord free worship?"

Back to Victorinus

10. No sooner had I heard Simplician's tale of Victorinus than I was on fire to do as he did—and no wonder: that is why he had told it to me. And he followed this up later with an account of how Victorinus, when Christians were forbidden by edict to teach literature and rhetoric in the time of the Emperor Julian, eagerly accepted the ban, preferring to leave the prattling schools for your Word, which 'makes even the tongues of wordless babes eloquent.' I thought him more relieved than reluctant in recognizing this opportunity to be entirely free to serve you, since I was yearning for just that thing. But I was immobilized—less by another's static imposition than by my own static will. For the enemy had in thrall my power to choose, which he had used to make a chain for binding me. From evil choice an urge arises; and the urge, yielded to, becomes a compulsion; and the compulsion, unresisted, becomes a slavery—each link in this process connected with the others, which is why I call it a chain—and that chain had a tyrannical grip around me. The new will I felt stirring in me, a will to 'give you free worship' and enjoy what I yearned for, my God, my only reliable happiness, could not break away from the will made strong by long dominance. Two wills were mine, old and new, of the flesh, of the spirit, each warring on the other, and between their dissonances was my soul disintegrating.

11. So by experiment upon myself I was coming to realize

L1 *the desire of the flesh*] Galatians 5.17: "The desire of the flesh opposes the spirit, the desire of the spirit opposes the flesh."

L5 *more identified with*] *Magis ego* here, with *magis ego* and *ex magna parte* in the next sentence. The contending wills in Augustine are contending identities, since "for Augustine the *velle* [willing] and the self are nearly identical" (O 3.34).

L6 *what I did not will*] Romans 7.16–17: If I do what I do not will . . . it is not I but the power of sin working within me."

L8 *willed I . . . nilled I*] To reproduce the tight paradox *volens quo nollem.*

L14 *loss . . . load*] To reproduce the play on *expediri . . . impediri.*

L21 *time to be rising*] Romans 13.11: "knowing that it is time, the hour is here, for you to be rising from sleep."

L25 *Awake, sleeper*] Ephesians 5.14: "Awake, sleeper, rise from the dead, and Christ will bring you light."

what I had read of, how 'the desire of the flesh opposes the spirit, the desire of the spirit opposes the flesh,' for I was experiencing both—yet I felt more identified with that in me which I now wanted than with that in me that I found wanting. But, no, I was not more identified with it, since more of me went along with 'what I did not will, than went along with what I willed.' Yet it was I myself who had made my compulsion my punisher, since willed I to go where nilled I to be—and what defense has a sinner if his punishment follows on his own acts? Nor could I plead at this point what had served as my earlier excuse—that I could not renounce the world to follow you while I was still undecided about your truth. Now I knew. But I balked at following your ensign, since I was in service to earthly things, and I feared more their loss when I should have feared more their load.

12.   It was a sweet load pressing on me, light as a dream-load, and the thoughts that I tried to direct toward you were like the struggles of those trying to wake, only to fall back into a depth of sleep. Though no one wants to sleep forever, realizing that wakefulness is the higher state, yet a man puts off waking when torpor, making heavy all his limbs, smothers him sweetly in slumber, against his better sense that 'it is time to be rising.' In that very way, though I knew that rising to your love were better than lapsing into my sloth, the former act had my approval and wish, the latter my pleasure and assent. No excuse was left me when you told me, 'Awake, sleeper, arise from the dead, and Christ will give you light.' I was defenseless when you urged your truth, since that truth I had already accepted. All I could mumble, muzzily, was: Later on. Or: Any moment now. Or: Wait a bit.

L2 *took an inner comfort*] Romans7.22–23: "I take an inner comfort in God's law, yet I see another law in my outer limbs, at war with my mind's law, taking me captive to the law of sin in my limbs."

L5 *leads and lords*] To reproduce the alliteration of *trahitur et tenetur.*

L6 *unwilling soul, willing to fall*] To reproduce the antithesis *invitus, volens.*

L7 *Who will deliver*] Romans 7.24–25: "Who will deliver me, in this pitiful state, from death's body, if not Jesus Christ, our Lord, through his bounty?"

L9 *testify to your honor*] Psalm 18.15: "I will testify to your honor, Lord, that it is solid."

L10 *my champion*] Psalm 18.15: "Lord, my champion and rescuer."

But the any-moment never came, and wait-a-bit stretched out to endless bits. It mattered little that 'I took an inner comfort in your law, since another law, that of my outer limbs, made war on my mind's law, and took me captive to the law of sin in my limbs.' Sin's law is the dominance of compulsion, which leads and lords it over the unwilling soul, willing to fall into such merited captivity. 'Who will deliver me, in this pitiful state, from death's body, if not Jesus Christ, our Lord, through his bounty?'

13.   I will tell what happened, and 'testify to your honor,' Lord, 'my champion and rescuer,' how you liberated me from the chains of carnal yearning tightly wrapped around me, and from the drudgery of my secular career. My now-ingrained panic was increasing daily, and I daily panted for you. I was spending in your church all the time I could spare from the clogging duties I resented. Alypius attended me, unemployed after his third term as assessor, waiting for clients to whom he could peddle legal service, as I was peddling eloquence (presuming that is vendible). Nebridius, who gave in to our friendly urgings, was helping Verecundus, our dear fellow, with his classes. Verecundus, a teacher in his native city of Milan, urgently wanted and asked for his due of friendship from our company, the help he badly needed. Nebridius, gentle and accommodating as he was, lent a hand not from any desire for pay (he could have earned more, had he wanted, from teaching on his own) but from unwillingness to deny us anything requested in the name of friendship. He did not advertise the help he gave, since he did not want to become known to people important by worldly standards, but tranquilly to devote as many hours as possible to the pursuit of wisdom by reading or conversing on the subject.

L2 *to our surprise*] To reflect Augustine's rare use of *ecce* when not quoting another—to suggest the accidental (that is providentel) nature of this triggering episode in his conversion. Note *repente* below.

L6 *gaming table*] It is the odd site for a Pauline text that explains Pontician's surprise when he opens the book, and again emphasizes the apparently chance way he is led to tell the conversion stories that follow.

L10 *at once*] *repente,* driving home the spontaneous "accident" of this intervention in Augustine's life.

Four More Converts:
Pontician's Friends and Their Wives

14. One day, while Nebridius was absent (I forget why), to our surprise a certain Pontician paid Alypius and me a visit at our dwelling place. He was our countryman, a fellow African, and an important official at the emperor's court. He had some request or other to make of us, and when we sat down to talk it over, he chanced to see a book that lay on our gaming table. He picked it up, opened it, and found, to his amazement, the letters of Saint Paul—he had expected it to be one of the books that had made my profession so wearisome to me. Smiling, looking intently at me, he was pleasantly surprised to find at once this of all books, and only this, at hand for my reading. For he was a Christian and had been baptized, one who knelt long and often, Lord, in prayer to you at your church. After I told him that I was closely studying Scripture, we engaged in a conversation during which he told me about Anthony, the Egyptian monk whose name was treasured by your servants, though we had never heard of him. When he learned this, he told us all about the great man, making up for our ignorance even as he wondered at it. It stunned us to hear what marvels you had wrought, marvels so recent, so almost contemporary. The whole company was astonished, we at hearing such wonders, he at our hearing them only now.

L5 *under Ambrose's care*] That Augustine did not know about Ambrose's sponsorship of this monastery shows how little he was attending to the bishop's activity (see Introduction).

L13 *poor in spirit*] Matthew 5.3: "Happy the poor in spirit, for they belong to the heavenly reign."

L14 *life of Anthony*] Augustine does not say here that the life being read, traditionally thought to be by Athanasius, tells of Anthony's own conversion to the eremitic life as a result of hearing certain words of scripture—Augustine is saving that for the key moment of his own conversion **[29]**.

L18 *members of the intelligence service*] These men were *agentes in rebus,* an elite corps, like Augustine's friend Evodius [T 9.17], who was later his fellow bishop.

L18 *suddenly*] The abruptness of conversion is emphasized throughout, creating the "myth of suddenness" discussed in the Introduction.

15. He expanded on the flocks of monasteries, the lives led there in your sweet service, the wild deserts made fertile—all of which was news to us. Even here at Milan, just outside the city walls, there was a monastery, populous with virtuous monks under Ambrose's care, that had escaped our attention. He pursued the matter, speaking as we listened in silent absorption. He told us how, once upon a time in Trier, he and three of his fellow officers, while the emperor was attending afternoon games at the circus, took a walk in the garden just outside the walls. They strolled in casual combinations, one ending up with Pontician, as it happened, and the other two drifting off together. Those two chanced in their walk on a house of some kind where your servants lived, 'poor in spirit, who belong to the heavenly reign.' They saw there a book containing the life of Anthony. As one of them began to read it, he was stunned and took fire, and even as he read began to consider taking up such a life himself, in service to you instead of the emperor (for they were both members of the intelligence service). Suddenly filled with holy love and a correcting shame, angry at himself, he looked at his friend and said: Please tell me what, with all our busy striving, we are trying to reach? Where are we going? What keeps us in service? Is it the highest post at court, as the emperor's intimates? But what distinction is more risky or unstable? How many perils will we have to face to reach a post of even greater peril? And how long must we labor to get there? Yet God's intimate I can become on the spot, merely by wanting to be.

Those were his words as, racked by the birth pangs of a

L11 *building their tower*] Luke 14.28, 33: "If one plans to build a tower, does he not sit down to estimate the cost? . . . so any of you who will not abandon everything he owns cannot be my disciple."

L24 *women to whom they were plighted*] This mention, at the very end of the story of the story, may look like a mere aside, but it is important to Augustine, as confirming his own view that his "conversion" must involve celibacy (see Introduction).

new self, he turned back to the book and, reading further, was changed in his depths where you behold him, and—as was soon made evident—his mind sloughed off the world. Still reading, he rode his veering heart, castigating himself until, after sifting the choices, he chose the true course. Now safely yours, he told his friend: I have wrenched myself free from our career and set myself to serve God alone. Now, on this spot, in this house, I begin. If you cannot join me, at least do not hinder me. But the other said he would join him in such a campaign for such a reward. Both of them, who now belonged to you, 'were building their tower at the estimated cost, of abandoning all their goods to follow you.' At this point Pontician, strolling with his companion elsewhere in the garden, sought the other two and, when they met, urged them to hurry back since night was falling. But those two told what they had decided and intended, how they had reached their decision and been confirmed in it, and requested, if the other pair did not wish to join them, not to hinder them. Pontician told us that he and his friend, while not abandoning their own careers, nonetheless wept over it, and gave their friends loyal encouragement, commending themselves to their prayers—then, with hearts dragging in the dust, they returned to the emperor's quarters, while the other two, with hearts fixed on heaven, stayed at that dwelling. When the women to whom they were plighted heard what had happened, they dedicated their own virginity to you.

16.   While Pontician was telling this story, you, Lord, used his words to wrench me around to front myself, dragging me out from behind my back, where I had cowered to avoid seeing

L1 *planting me*] Psalm 49.21: "I shall plant you before your own face."

L6 *look on my sinfulness*] Psalm 35.3: "lest he might look on his sinfulness and learn to hate it."

L18 *young man*] *Adolescens,* not our "adolescence," but covering the years sixteen to thirty.

L19 *youth's outset*] He had dated this at the beginning of Book II, when his sexual liaison began. He has gone back beyond his twenty-first year (reading *Hortensius*) to his sixteenth.

L23 *down deviant paths*] Ecclesiasticus 2.16: "those who have wandered from direct paths and gone down deviant paths."

L23 *blaspheming religion*] Manicheism.

L27 *put off*] Ecclesiasticus 5.8: "Delay not your conversion to the Lord, do not put it off, day after day."

myself, and 'planting me in front of my own face,' where I could see the foul me, how distorted and dirty, how spotted, how ulcerous. The sight revolted me, but there was no escaping it—each time I tried to turn my gaze away from me, he went on with his story; and you kept holding me there, thrusting me into my own face, so I might 'look on my sinfulness and learn to hate it.' I had known of it before, but I kept obscuring it, giving in, not remembering.

17.   At that point, however, the more I loved these men who, for spiritual health, surrendered themselves entirely into your healing hands, the more disgust I felt for myself, because of the contrast with them. Many years had drifted by me, a dozen or so, since that twenty-first year when I was inspired to seek wisdom by Cicero's *Hortensius*. I had put off the rejection of worldly joys to seek it alone, though even the seeking of wisdom, not to say winning it, is far better than winning earthly pleasure, political power over others, or sensual pleasures summoned at will. But I was pitiable as a young man, just as I had been at youth's outset, and I still petitioned you for chastity, saying: Give me chastity and self-control, but not just now. I was afraid you would hear me too soon, heal me too soon, from the sick urges I wanted rather intensified than terminated. I had 'gone down deviant paths' with the help of a false and blaspheming religion, which I did not so much accept as true as prefer to others I was not virtuous enough to pursue but viciously resisted.

18.   When I 'put off, day after day,' the decision to spurn worldly hope and seek you alone, the reason, I thought, was

L11 *and I went in*] The two motions linked by the chiasmus *abiit ille et ego* [*inii*] *ad me*. A good example of Augustine's kinetic treatment of the knowing process.

L13 *verbal reverberations*] *Verber* (lash for beating) is actually related to *verbena* (stick), but Augustine linked it with *verbum,* since a word "beats" the ear (*The Teacher* 12).

that I was not certain what was the right path to take. But the day had now arrived when I was naked to myself, and my conscience rebuked me, asking: What have you to say now? Till now you used to claim that you could not escape involvement with hollow things because you were not sure of the right course. But now you are sure, and yet are still encumbered—while wings have long since lifted free men's shoulders, who did not spend ten years and more considering if they should fly.

In this way was I gnawed within, was I stalled in a terrible regret, as Pontician was telling his story. When he had finished, and concluded the errand he had come on, he went away and I went in, in to myself, and what complaints against myself did I omit? With what verbal reverberations I lashed my soul, trying to force it after me in my quest for you. But it balked, it would not move, though it could not excuse itself—all its arguments had run out, had been refuted. It could only tremble in silence, thinking it were death to escape the stream of habits draining it to death.

The Garden

19.   In this great wracking of my inner habitation, which I had provoked against my soul in the intimate straits I shared with it, I went to Alypius with storm on my face and in my mind, and burst out: What is the matter with us? Has it come to this? Did you hear that story? Non-philosophers surge ahead of us and snatch heaven, while we, with our cold learning—we, just look at us—are still mired in flesh and blood. Just because they have got ahead, should we be ashamed to follow *at all*, rather be shamed *at least* into following?

I said something or other of this sort, before my seethings tore me away from him, while he could only stare at me in a stunned silence, so little sense were my words making, as my frown, grimace, eyes, pallor, and tone of voice said more of what I was feeling than any words could. There was a garden where we were staying, which was at our disposal, like the entire house, since our host, the home owner, was not in residence. Thither my inner turmoil carried me, where no one could interfere with my inner conflagration before its outcome was decided—in a way you foreknew, but I did not; since I was now crazed to be sane, was dying to be alive, aware of how bad things were with me, unaware of how good they were shortly to become.

l.5 *deeply moved*] John 11.33: "[Jesus] was deeply moved within himself."

l.6 *made my promised compact*] Ezekiel 16.8: "The Lord God said, 'I have made a pact with you.' "

l.7 *my very bones*] Psalm 34.10: "My very bones will say, 'Who is your like?' "

l.8 *no ship or carriage*] Plotinus, *The Nines* 1.6.8: "Let us fly back to the homeland ... by what vehicle of escape? We do not need to walk ... nor to employ a carriage-and-team, nor any kind of ship." A favorite passage of Augustine's.

As I went into the garden, Alypius followed close on my heels, staying with me though not sharing my inner condition—but how could he leave me alone in such a state? We sat down as far away from the buildings as we could. I was 'deeply moved within myself,' outrage provoking deeper outrage, with sadness that I had not 'made my promised compact with you, my God,' though 'my very bones cried out' for making it, for honoring it in heaven. But where I was going 'no ship or carriage or walking could take me,' though where I was going was not even as far as I had come from the house. Not only going there but arriving there was simply a matter of willing it—but willing it with a strong and unified will, not a partial and wounded will, one jerking and lunging, part of it surging, part sinking.

20. As I thrashed about, resisting, I made the bodily motions of persons who would if they could *do* something, but cannot—either because they lack a limb, or because the limb is tied up, withered by illness, or otherwise debilitated. Yet I, when tearing my hair, pounding my head, hugging tight my knee with laced fingers, was doing with my body exactly what I willed—the willing would not have been followed by this effect if my limbs' response had been blocked. Yet I could not do what I far more eagerly wanted to do, and which I should have been able to do at will, since what I wanted to do at will was—to will. Here the faculty to be affected by the will was itself. And what it had to do was to be itself. Yet it could not. My body's limbs were moved by the soul's lightest volition, receiving its direc-

tion, yet the soul did not respond to its own eager willing, when all it had to perform was to will.

21.   Why this enormity, whence arises it? May your pity shed light on the matter as I enquire if the answer may lie in the secret penalties and dark remorses of descent from Adam. Is the enormity there? Thence does it arise? The mind commands, and the body is prompt to respond. The mind commands itself, and it is defied. The mind commands the hand to move, and is so much in charge that the command is hardly different from the response, though the mind is a mental reality, the hand a corporal one. Yet when the mind orders the mind, they are one and the same—and the command is not carried out. Why such enormity, whence arises it, I repeat, that the mind commands the will to respond, and would not order it if it did not will to do so, yet the command is not obeyed. Is it that the will is half-hearted, so the command is halfhearted? The intensity of the command comes from the intensity of the will to make it, and if the will fails to obey the command, that shows a lack of intensity in the will that gave the command. The will that commands is the same will that is commanded—no other is being commanded. The command must therefore be halfhearted if it is not carried out. If it were wholehearted, it would not have to issue the command, it would already have the will. There is no such enormity, then, as simultaneously willing and not willing. Rather there is a sickness of the soul, weighed down by compulsions that impede its response to the truth. In that sense there are two wills, each halfhearted, each lacking what the other has.

L1 *Let them fade*] Psalm 67.3: "So let sinners fade away from the gaze of God."

L1 *empty talkers*] Titus 5.8: "Many are disobedient, the empty talkers and per-verters."

L2 *assenting . . . assert*] For *animadverterint . . . adseverant.*

L4 *two minds in a man*] Augustine is still arguing with his former Maniche-ism. As O'Donnell notes here, "The ferocity of his opposition testifies that Augustine always felt the force of Manichean arguments" (O 3.48).

L6 *hold . . . hold close*] For *senserint . . . consenserint.*

L7 *Once you were darkness*] Ephesians 5.8: "Once you were darkness, now in the Lord you are light."

L11 *the true light*] John 1.9: "the true light that illumines each man as he comes into the world."

L13 *coming to him*] Psalm 33.6: "Come to him for the light and your faces shall not blush."

L20 *no longer I that acted*] Romans 7.17: "I am no longer acting but the sin that is within me."

L22 *freely sinning*] Augustine thought only Adam's sin was an entirely free act, since all later wills were perverted by his "original sin."

22.   'Let them fade from your gaze,' God—as the 'empty talkers and mind's perverters' fade from it—who, assenting that there can be two wills hesitating over a decision, assert that there are two minds in a man, one of them good, one not. Men become evil holding such evil views, just as it will make them virtuous if they not only hold right views but hold close to their truth—as your apostle tells them, 'Once you were darkness, now in the Lord you are light.' Those who wish to be light in themselves, not in the Lord, become a deeper darkness, holding that the nature of their souls is itself God—which carries them off from you into a terrible pride, farther off from 'the true light that illumines each man as he comes into this world.' Let them pay attention to your words, and blush, since 'coming to him for the light, you shall not blush.'

But I, in my hesitation over whether to serve the Lord at last, as I had long been disposed to do, was the same man willing as was nilling, both were me. For my willing was as half-hearted as my nilling. I was at war within, was exiled from myself. My exile was unwelcome to me, caused not by a second nature in me but by the cost of sin. For it was 'no longer I that acted but the sin within me,' my lot as Adam's son, and the price of his freely sinning.

23.   If different wills make for different natures in man, there would not be two such but many. If a person is trying to decide whether to go to a Manichean gathering or to the theater, the Manicheans will cry out: Here are two natures, a good one drawn in one direction, an evil one in the other, producing the suspension of action between contending wills. If I say that

both intentions—to attend their service and go to the theater—
are evil, they answer that their meetings can only be good. But
if one of our faith is of two minds about attending the theater
or our own church, must the Manicheans not be of two minds
how to describe the situation? Either they must say, unwill-
ingly, that our intention of going to church is a good one (as
indeed it is for those who are baptized and hold to the sacra-
mental life), or that the struggle within a single man is in this
case a struggle between wills that are both bad—and that is
enough to confute their claim that the two wills in man are always a good one and a bad one. Their only alternative is to be
converted to the truth, that when one hesitates over a decision,
he is tossed about by the conflict of various intentions.

24.   Therefore, when they observe two intentions at odds
with each other in a man, they have no grounds for saying that
two substantially different natures are in conflict, reflecting
opposed principles in the universe, the good against the bad.
For you, the true God, can blame and out-argue and over-
whelm them, since in deciding whether to commit murder
with poison or a knife, both intentions are evil; as are the intentions to cheat this man or that man of his property, when one
cannot do both; or the intentions to spend money in lust or
hoard money in greed. Shall I spend my time going to the
games or to a drama, when only one can be chosen because
they are playing simultaneously—or, to add a third option,
shall I rather rob this house or that (given opportunity to do
both); or, a fourth option, shall I commit adultery when that,
too, becomes an opportunity on offer? Add them all up, as op-

L16 *admiring . . . mired*] To approximate the punning bathos of *praeponit . . . ponit.*

L18 *So sick . . . than before*] Augustine's grammar tosses about in this long, loosely constructed, and entrammeling sentence. A good case of moral quandary *reenacted* in language.

L19 *churning and chafing*] To reproduce the alliteration of *volvens et versans me in vinculo.*

tions simultaneously offered, all tempting though all cannot be indulged, and the will is scattered out among four or more different things it wants, yet they do not say there are as many different natures as desires in a single man.

The same variations can be found in good intentions. If I ask the Manicheans, Is it more virtuous to savor the words of the apostle, or to savor a correcting psalm, or to analyze a gospel text, they will answer that each one is virtuous. But if all these seem equally attractive at any one time, will these contending possibilities not confuse the mind while it considers which we should prefer? All are good, but they compete with each other until one of them is chosen and the will can concentrate on it alone, no longer toying with the others. In this way, when the higher delights of heaven lift us, but the joys of temporal existence drag us back, the mind is not totally concentrated on one or the other, admiring the higher for its truth but mired by habit in the lower.

25.   So sick was I, so tortured, as I reviled myself more bitterly than ever, churning and chafing in my chains, not broken free of them entirely, held more loosely now, but still held, as you were working in my hidden places, with your fierce pity wielding the double whip of fear and shame to prevent my relapse, to prevent the loosening and lighter bond that still held me from renewing its grip, to grapple me again more tightly than before. My inner self was urging me: Make it now! Make it now! With those words I was moving to a resolution, I was almost there—but was not there. Still, I did not slide all the way back, but braced myself nearby, catching my breath; then,

L1 *almost . . . almost . . . all but . . . all but*] In contrast to the long entrammeling sentence above, the short, panting, resurgent phrases show repeated shoves outward from the net.

L4 *engrained . . . untrained*] To reproduce the chiming antithesis *inolitum* (en) . . . *insolitum.*

L10 *entrenched lusts*] O'Donnell shows that former *(veteres)* lovers are not being referred to, but Augustine's own entrenched (*antiquae,* "of long standing") desires (O 3.52–53).

L17 *tittering . . . picking*] O'Donnell notes the colloquialism of the terms, something more than "whispering" and "pulling" (O 3.53).

renewing the effort, I almost made it—almost—but did not; I was all but touching, all but clasping—but no, I was not there, not yet touching, not yet clasping, not ready to die to death and live to life, still held by the engrained evil in me over the untrained good in me. The moment when I would become someone different, the closer it came, the more terror it struck in me—a terror, however, that no longer wrenched me back or fended me off, but just left me hanging.

26. The triflingest of things, the very hollowest things of the hollow-headed, had stalled me—my entrenched lusts, plucking me back by my fleshly clothing, whispering low: Can you cast us off? And: From this moment, never more to be with us! And: From this moment, never to do this, not ever, or to do this! What they specified by "this" and "this," keep far from me, God—what sordid, what disgraceful things they spelled out for me. Yet I less than half adverted to their words, since they no longer flaunted themselves in my path, but were tittering behind me, as if furtively picking at me while I pulled away from them, trying to make me look back. And held in some measure I was, not willing to break off, to reject them finally, to cast myself forward to what was calling me. And harsh old compulsion was all the while saying, Can you live without them?

27. Yet even its words were fading. Off in the direction I was turned to, though afraid to advance into it, Lady Self-Control was revealed in all her chaste majesty, serene, quietly mirthful, smiling me on to come near, not to hold back. To welcome and to hug me she reached her holy arms out, and in

L4 *mother fertile*] Psalm 112.9: "He makes the home's sterile woman fertile, happy in her children."

L15 *let them be deadened*] Colossians 3.5: "Make your limbs dead to the things of this earth."

them were throngs of models setting me an example, innocent
boys and girls, young men and women—all ages, including
chaste widows and women still virgin in their youth. In all of
them, Self-Control was not sterile but 'a mother fertile with
children of happiness' by you, Lord, her husband. She teased
me with a smiling insistence: Can you not do what all of these
have? Or do you think they did it by themselves, without God
their Lord? He it was who gave me to them. Why do you stand
alone, which is no standing at all? Throw yourself on him! Do
you think he will not stay your fall? Give up fear, and throw
yourself—he will catch you, and will heal you.

I was profuse with blushings, since I still had an ear for the
insinuations of the triflers, I was still hanging there in irresolu-
tion. But she went on saying, as it were: Deafen yourself 'to
your earthly limbs, let them be deadened'—they promise delights, but not the delights of the Lord your God's law.

This battle in my heart pitted me and no other against myself, while Alypius, loyal at my side, could only wait in silence
for explanation of this weird behavior.

28.   By looking thus deep into myself I dragged from my
inmost hiding places my entire store of pitiable memories and
laid them out for my heart to look on. A vast storm hit me
at this point, and brought great sheets of showering tears.
To retch this all completely out of me, I leaped away from
Alypius—I needed to be alone for this labor of weeping—and I
moved farther off, where not even his presence could inhibit
me. He honored what was happening to me—perhaps it appeared from my voice, broken with sobs, as I said something

L3 *headlong*] Literally, "any which way" *(nescio quomodo)*, without giving thought to proper custody of his body motions (important in antiquity). Augustine stresses his lack of control over the throes of his ordeal.

L3 *fig tree*] For symbolic meaning see Introduction and [*comm.*].

L3 *loosing the reins*] Virgil, *Aeneid* 12.499: "He loosed all reins to his wrath."

L6 *how much more?*] Psalm 6.4: "How much more, Lord?"

L7 *until your anger is exhausted*] Psalm 78.5: "How much more, Lord, until your anger is exhausted?"

L8 *heed no more*] Psalm 78.8: "Heed no more, I pray, my entrenched vices."

L15 *Lift! Look!*] Translated for double meaning described in Introduction and [*comm.*].

L19 *by divine prompting*] Athanasius (?), *Life of Saint Anthony:* "a thing by divine prompting read just for him" [*comm.*].

or other. At any rate, I leaped away. He, in a state of extreme shock, remained where we sat down, while I leaped up and headlong threw myself down under some fig tree, 'loosing the reins to my sobbing,' as tears tore themselves from my eyes, my condign offering to you as I multiplied my laments, not exactly in these words but to this effect: 'Lord, how much more?' 'How much more, Lord, until your anger is exhausted?' 'Heed no more, I pray, my entrenched vices.'

I felt still in the grip of those vices, and I blubbered pitiably: How long, how long—on the morrow is it, always the morrow? Why never now? Why is not now the termination point of my sins?   29.   I was carrying on so, crying acrid tears of heart's contrition, when, of a sudden, I heard from a nearby house the voice of a boy—or perhaps a girl, I could not tell—chanting in repeated singsong: Lift! Look! My features relaxed immediately while I studied as hard as I could whether children use such a chant in any of their games. But I could not remember ever having heard it. No longer crying, I leaped up, not doubting that it was 'by divine prompting' that I should open a book and read what first I hit on.

L1 *chanced to be present*] Athanasius (?), *Life of Saint Anthony II:* "He entered church, where by chance a certain passage of scripture was read."

L4 *Go, sell*] Matthew 19.21: "If you wish for completion, go, sell all you own, give it to the poor, and you will have heavenly treasure—only come, and follow me."

Seventh Conversion Story: Anthony

For I had heard how Anthony, though he merely 'chanced to be present when a certain passage of scripture was read,' nonetheless took it to heart as meant specifically for him when he heard: 'Go, sell all you own, give it to the poor, and you will have heavenly treasure—only come, and follow me.' At this divine signal he was suddenly converted to you.

L3 *Give up indulgence*] Romans 13.13: "Give up indulgence and drunkenness, give up lust and obscenity, give up strife and rivalries, and clothe yourself in Jesus Christ the Lord, leaving no further allowance for fleshly desires."

L14 *Welcome him*] Romans 14.1: "Welcome him whose faith is weak, without intellectual disputes."

L22 *can act beyond*] Ephesians 3.20: "who can act far beyond what we ask or conceive."

Eighth Conversion Story: Augustine

I rushed back to where Alypius was sitting, since there I had left the book of the apostle when I leaped up from him. I snatched, opened, read: 'Give up indulgence and drunkenness, give up lust and obscenity, give up strife and rivalries, and clothe yourself in Jesus Christ the Lord, leaving no further allowance for fleshly desires.' The very instant I finished that sentence, light was flooding my heart with assurance, and all my shadowy reluctance evanesced.

30.   I closed the book, marking the place with my finger or something, and spoke to Alypius with a countenance now calmed, after which he spoke to me of what he was undergoing without my knowing it. He asks what I had read. I showed him, and he goes beyond what I had read in the passage, to the part I had not seen, where it ran: 'Welcome him whose belief is weak.' The words exactly applied to his condition, as he showed me. He was braced by this encouragement, and it took no turbulence of resistance for him to join me in the promised compact with you, since in the moral purity called for he had long been my better.

From there we go to my mother; speak with her; she rejoices. We give her the details of what happened. It is joy and glory to her, and she was thanking you, 'who can act beyond l.5 *ruler's edge*] This refers to Monnica's dream, when Augustine was still a Manichean. She stood along a ruler's edge, weeping for her son's heresy, when a young man appeared and asked her to look behind her along the ruler, where she saw Augustine standing (T 3.19–20).

l.6 *changed her grieving*] Psalm 29.12: "You have changed my grieving into my joy."

what we ask or think is possible,' since she saw you had granted her far more than she had asked with her pitiable long laments for me. You had so converted me to you that you freed me from seeking a wife or any other prospect of this world. I was standing at last on that ruler's edge of faith where you had shown me to her years ago. 'You changed her grieving into joy,' far beyond her intentions—with a chaster, sweeter joy than she had looked for from grandchildren born of me.

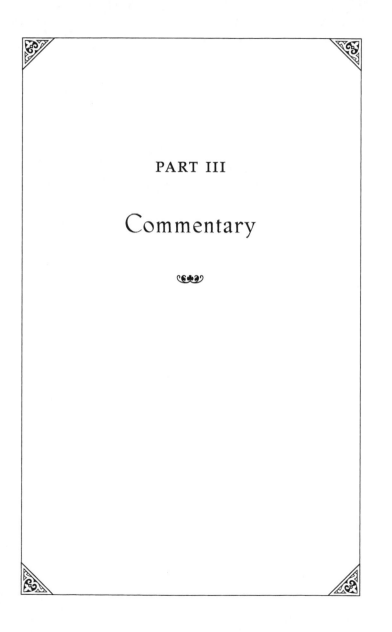

PART III

Commentary

1.   Augustine says at the outset of this book that his two last intellectual problems had been surmounted. He now believed that God is eternal, and that he is immaterial. These have been firmly entrenched in the casings of his heart *(praecordium)* and in the outer walls of his castle *(circumvalla)*. But the moral concomitants of the two problems have not been solved. He is still in time, and therefore unstable; and he is still mired in lust, and to that extent far from God's immateriality.

The determination to seek counsel from Simplician, the leader of the Christian Neoplatonists in Milan, comes from Augustine's inability to get any help from Ambrose, who was too busy to confer with Augustine in any but a perfunctory way (T 6.3–4). Simplician had not only been Ambrose's own sponsor in the faith—baptizing him when he was called to be bishop, and then succeeding him in that office—but his mentor in Neoplatonic readings of Scripture. Augustine was going to the source, prompted (he says) by the leadings of grace. But Augustine does not want intellectual arguments now, but moral guidance from a skilled leader of the soul, one who like the wise man who can bring both old and new vintages from his store of wisdom (Matthew 13.52). It is this metaphor that Augustine relies on when, as a bishop himself, he writes an answer to a letter of Simplician: "The heartfelt affection you show in your letter is not a new and untried vintage to me, but a familiar and treasured taste brought up from the cellar" (Epistle 37.1).

2.   What are the things Augustine would "be forced to put up with" in marriage *(pati cogebar)*? We meet here the ascetical views that were sweeping not only Christian but Jewish and pagan circles, particularly intellectual circles, in the fourth century—for which see Peter Brown's indispensable *Body and Society*. This exciting rush to asceticism led to the cult of desert fathers and holy virgins, to the first widespread introduction of celibacy in the Christian clergy, and to the belief that *sex could be indulged in marriage only as necessary for the production of offspring*. This is the view of marriage Augustine would celebrate when discussing such married semicelibates as Paulinus of Nola, Pinian, and the father of Julian of Eclanum. It was the code he would try to enforce in his flock. But it was a code that Augustine, being realistic about his own sexual appetite, thought he could not observe in marriage. He could not be close to a wife, as he had been close to Adeodatus' mother for a decade and a half, and have sex with her only when there was a realistic prospect of begetting further children. This was not a matter of fidelity in marriage—he said that in all his time with his loved consort, he had been "true to her bed alone" (T 4.2). But their sex was unrestricted by the need for offspring—they had only the one child, and that by accident, early on.

No sex at all seemed safer for Augustine than sex under such constant temptation and such constant inhibition—it was a matter of all or nothing. But no sex at all also looked impossible for him **[26]**. By the standards of the day, when there was nothing like what would later be known as the sacrament of penance, serious sin after baptism could be forgiven only once, after public confession and difficult probation. After that, one was excluded from the Christian community. This had been the reason Augustine's baptism was delayed in the first place, to allow him a period of indulgence before accepting such a hard commitment (T 1.18). This psychosexual quandary is the thing that must be addressed successfully in the garden scene—which shows how narrow and idiosyncratic was the "conversion" enacted there. He would have to make himself a eunuch for the heavenly reign—but he read the gospel's words, "Claim it who can," and had to answer in all honesty, "I can't."

3.   Since Augustine says that he had been reading the Neoplatonists before he went to Simplician, that may mean that Mallius Theodore (with whom Augustine read the philosophers) introduced the two, rather than that Simplician steered Augustine to Theodore. In the dedication to *Happiness in This Life*, Augustine says that he and Theodore had discussions with "our priest" *(presbyter noster)*, meaning Simplician. These discussions probably had to do with intellectual matters. But now (at least in the *Testimony* account) Augustine is coming to Simplician for moral guidance. He presents it as a first meeting with him, since he wants to exclude Theodore from *The Testimony*—Theodore had disappointed Augustine on the point he most admired in him, his surrender of a worldly career, when he went back into the emperor's service.

Simplician expertly diagnoses Augustine's needs, and deliberately tells him the story that most applies to his own situation. Victorinus was also convinced of the Christian truths, but would not take the step of baptism because he did not want to give up the worldly honors of his position. Augustine tells us that he had given up desire for those honors [2]; but he was held back by a different kind of worldliness, by desires of the flesh. The example of Victorinus' humility in confessing error publicly and making his profession of belief is meant to prod Augustine into asking humbly for a similar grace. All the stories of conversion in this book are either intended by their tellers, or by God in providentially putting them in Augustine's way, to shape a journey into and through the garden of "conversion." The usefulness of the Victorinus story is emphasized, to the point where the actual contact of Augustine with any translation by Victorinus is left problematic.

Augustine, who never met Victorinus, tells us only what he learned about him from Simplician, who did know him. O'Donnell rightly says (O 3.12) that the persuasive use made of Victorinus to motivate Augustine toward baptism, and the possible exaggerations by Augustine to bring out that persuasive point, are not the best guides to what Victorinus was really like or what he actually did. Saint Jerome knew Victorinus well, since he had been his pupil, and what he has to say of him is not complimentary. He mentions him three times:

> Victorinus the rhetorician, and my [other] teacher Donatus the grammarian, had high reputations in Rome, and Victori-

nus even earned from some a statue in the Forum of Trajan (*Chronicle* 7).

I am aware, as well, that Caius Marius Victorinus, who taught me rhetoric in my youth at Rome, published commentaries on the apostle [Paul], but because of his absorption in the fine points of secular literature he completely neglected the sacred texts, and no one, no matter what his eloquence, can explain well what he does not know" (*Comm. Gal.*, Preface).

Victorinus, an African by birth, who taught rhetoric in Rome when Constantine was emperor, devoted himself to the Christian faith in his old age; besides commentaries on the apostle, he wrote books against Arius—which are, however, so obscured by a polemical approach that only experts could follow them (*Famous Men* 101).

Augustine has caused endless wrangling over what Platonic texts he read, made all the more difficult by the fact that the one such text he specifies did not, apparently, exist. Jerome lists no Platonic translations among the works of Victorinus, and neither does anyone else. Moreover, Augustine never once cites the actual words of Victorinus, or of any translation by Victorinus. Is he just tying Victorinus closely to his own conversion because of the push Simplician gave him, using the Victorinus story? This should make us wary of any literalist approach to Augustine's conversion. He is remembering the action of grace *through* worldly events and almost *in spite of* them.

6. Augustine seems to entertain a diversion here—asking why there is more joy for the desperate soul rescued than for the soul that always stayed true to the Lord. It is the thing that has puzzled people in the story of the prodigal son—why is the strayed one treated better than the brother who never strayed? Augustine's answer is in two parts. First, the sheer relief of escape from danger makes people treasure more what they took for granted when it was not in danger. After giving examples of this psychological maxim, spanning a broad range from illicit to licit to supernatural joys [7–8], Augustine adds (in [9]) an evangelist's explanation where the reclaiming of sinners is at issue. As leaders of revivals note, the hope raised in others is often greater if it can be shown that a sinner as great as or greater than they has been saved. This is especially true if the rescued person is a celebrity, whose condition will be better known to more people than would that of an obscure person. Victorinus was a prize. The acceptability of such celebrity "head hunting" is emphasized by Augustine's peculiar reading of Acts 13.7–12—Saul had been so proud to wrest a proconsul from the clutches of a Jewish sorcerer (Bar-Jesus) that he took the convert's name (Paul) as a sign of victory. It was probably the parallel between Victorinus' evil celebration of gods like Anubis and the magic spells of Bar-Jesus that made Augustine invoke this conversion-story-within-a-conversion-story. In one sense, it does not fit with the other stories used in the book. Like the conversion of Saul himself, it involves accepting the Christian faith, instead of a special vocation within that faith.

7.   Augustine's comparison of great with little things is seen when he uses the hedonist's way of provoking thirst with things like victory after a hard battle. The desire to cultivate feelings of relief has been noted by others. Benjamin Haydon wrote of his friend, the poet John Keats: "He once covered his tongue and throat as far as he could reach with Cayenne pepper, in order to appreciate the delicious coolness of claret in all its glory—his own expression" (Tom Taylor, editor, *The Life of Benjamin Robert Haydon, From His Autobiography and Journals*, London, 1853, vol. 2, p. 9). To this day, bartenders put out free peanuts and other salty food to encourage people to buy more drinks.

9.   The story of Sergius Paul is told at Acts 13.6–12:

> They [Paul, Barnabas, John] traversed the whole island as far as Paphos, where they encountered a Jewish magician and pseudo-prophet, Bar-Jesus by name, an attendant on the governor, Sergius Paul, a man of understanding. He had sent for Barnabas and Saul from a desire to hear the word of God. But the magician Elymas (to translate his name) opposed them, wishing to prevent the conversion *(diastrepsai)* of the governor. But Saul, also called Paul, glaring at him in an afflatus of the Holy Spirit, said: You expert in every fraud and trickery, son of the devil and foe of all virtue, will you never stop making the Lord's straight ways crooked? Here is the Lord's hand on you, to strike you blind, unable for a while to see sunlight. At the word a cloud and darkness involved him, and he groped around for a hand to lead him. The governor, when he saw this deed, believed, stunned by what was revealed of the Lord.

As was noted in the Introduction, this is the only story of conversion to the faith in all of Book Eight, and it is brought in only by the way, to show the efficacy of converting prominent people. Since this is the first mention in Acts of Saul's other name, Paul, Augustine thinks Paul renamed himself for the prize he bagged—which fits better his thesis, at this point, on the importance of celebrity conversions, than it fits anything in Luke's text.

10–12.   These paragraphs offer a psychologically acute description of the growth of an addiction, and the feeling of helplessness experienced by its victim. It shows why Book Eight is so popular with people who have experienced such addiction and have taken the steps needed to escape from it. It may seem odd that Augustine, who has told us that his intellectual difficulties had been resolved by this point, should pause at the climax of his conversion narrative to *argue* again—with opponents of free will here, and with the Manichean doctrine of the two wills at [21–25]. But he is dealing with his own moral quandary precisely by isolating it from the false quandaries presented to him in the past. His paralysis of will is not explicable, any more, in terms of a denial of free will. And the presence of contending wills in him can no longer be submitted to as a necessary consequence of a divided nature, which is how Manicheans explained it.

On free will, he argues that addiction shows not the absence of free will, but its misuse. The will can use its powers in a suicidal way, weakening itself by its own force when it makes a series of choices that progressively narrow its choices. He presents this paradox in a play on *volens-nolens* language climaxed in the pithy *volens quo nollem perveneram,* "willed I to go where nilled I to be" **[11]**.

13.   It is not immediately apparent why Verecundus should be introduced here into the narrative. But Augustine is setting up a network of friendships that will correspond to the network of friendship exemplified in Pontician's immediately following and crucial account of the four friends (and their two affianced women) in Trier. Augustine's final struggle in the garden, when he separates himself even from his closest friend Alypius, may give the impression that his conversion was an entirely private and single action. But he means to show that grace acts within the social framework. Even sin came into the world by a perverse social sense, the *socialis necessitudo* that made Adam retain his solidarity with Eve (First Meanings in Genesis 14.11). Redemption also has a communal aspect. The generosity of Verecundus, based on his sense of duty to his friends, is a happier kind of *socialis necessitudo,* which will be continued when he offers his villa at Cassiciacum to the community of his friends. But Adam's original social compulsion will also be demonstrated in Verecundus, when he refuses to join the company because of his tie to a wife (T 9.5). Augustine was operating within a social texture that both strengthened and weakened him in his struggle of the will. This ambivalent situation will be demonstrated by Pontician's story when two of the four men being described are unable to follow the heroic choice of their other companions, however much they admire it.

14. Pontician first tells Augustine about the hermit Anthony—but Augustine deliberately refrains from repeating at this point what he was told. He simply remarks that it was odd that he had not heard of this famous man, and that Pontician noted the oddity. It is providential that Augustine should be learning the story just when it would prove most helpful to him. But precisely because it will be so useful, Augustine puts off giving us the content of the tale. It will be "remembered" at the point where it provides the closest parallel to Augustine's own conversion—when he reflects that Anthony, too, was converted by a passage from Scripture [29]. This withholding of the "punch line" shows how carefully Augustine is arranging his conversion accounts to focus with increasing relevance on his own final step.

15. This long paragraph, with Pontician's second story (after that of Anthony), moves from a consideration of the single excellence of hermits to the happy life in "flocks" *(greges)* of monastic saints. The power of example is strong here with Augustine, since he always envisaged that his life as a Christian would involve membership in a community of learned celibates. For him, it was not a matter of his single salvation but of a philosophical discipline jointly pursued with others. The first approximation to this was the failed attempt to found such a company in his pre-baptismal days (T 6.24). The second would be the "seminar" at Cassiciacum. The third would be his exercises in dialogue with Erodius and Alypius. But only in Hippo would he finally bring together the partners he needed to pursue the Christian life in community. That is the promise

held out by the holy companions of Trier. The missing aspect in their company was learning; but the vocation to poverty resembled in Augustine's mind the philosopher's distancing of himself from worldly concerns. To disencumber the mind of temporal connections was the first step toward wisdom in the thought of Late Antiquity. In this sense, praise of the four holy companions (two men, two women) at Trier was a more enticing model for Augustine than any of the other conversion stories—those of Victorinus, of Sergius Paul, of Anthony, or even of Paul himself.

There is another aspect to this tale, brought out in the speech of the first man to be inspired to monasticism when he turns to his friend. The speech, it should be noted, is Augustine's own, since Pontician was not present to hear it. It is a fiction within a secondhand narrative. What Augustine supplies in this place is tailored for its specific relevance to him—a point made clear when Augustine turns to his own friend and speaks in a similar vein. He admits that even this latter speech is not exactly reported—"I said something or other of this sort." The two speeches are not exact, then, but they are exactly appropriate, as shaped by Augustine's artistry. Here is the first:

> Suddenly filled with holy love and a correcting shame, angry at himself, he looked at his friend and said: Please tell me what, with all our busy striving, we are trying to reach? Where are we going? What keeps us in service? Is it the highest post at court, as the emperor's intimates? But what distinction is more risky or unstable? How many perils will we have to face to

reach a post of even greater peril? And how long must we labor to get there? Yet God's intimate I can become on the spot, merely by wanting to be.

Here is the second:

I went to Alypius with storm on my face and in my mind, and burst out: What is the matter with us? Has it come to this? Did you hear that story? Non-philosophers surge ahead of us and snatch heaven, while we, with our cold learning—we, just look at us—are still mired in flesh and blood. Just because they have got ahead, should we be ashamed to follow *at all,* rather be shamed *at least* into following?

Though one speaker is struggling to give up worldly advancement, and the other is struggling to give up worldly attractions of the flesh, there is in both a *competitive* piety that can jar with some. Augustine, who wants to be an ascetical star, is shamed by the unlearned who press in before him. This part of *The Testimony* is certainly true to what he was writing at the time of his conversion, when he aimed at a "deifying" life of contemplation. Augustine will in time outgrow this purely intellectual ideal of Christian life, but he has not entirely done so even in the year 397, when he composed *The Testimony*.

21–24.   Augustine is still disturbed enough about the force of Manichean arguments that he takes three full paragraphs to prevent his inner division from being mistaken for the condition the Manicheans made central to their psychological appeal.

They played a role in Late Antiquity somewhat like that of Freud in the twentieth century—making people aware of unsuspected or partly masked inner conflicts. Augustine reduces their two-natures argument to absurdity by first simplifying what they said and then destroying this straw man. In his version, the Manicheans believed that there were two (and only two) contending wills in each person, one good and one bad. The Manicheans could answer that these were two ultimate orientations, which might be engaged only occasionally or partially under the shifting desires or impulses of the moment. Augustine himself would espouse something like this when he saw the conflict between the City of God and the City of Man, sometimes recruiting this, sometimes that, aspect of a person or a society.

Nonetheless, Augustine is speaking from the complexity of his own situation, as he describes it in the garden scene, and he reasonably says that the Manicheans would very likely explain that in too rigid a way. At any rate, Augustine makes three arguments against what he presents as Manichean doctrine, as that doctrine might be imagined by an individual in psychological turmoil. Augustine says: (1) The Manicheans stress the existence of two wills, one bad and one good, but there can in fact be *many* contending desires or intentions, reflecting as many wills. (2) And even when there are many wills, in any concrete situation, all of them might be intended toward good objects. (3) Or, contrariwise, they might all be intending evil. Though he simplifies the matter for rebuttal purposes, he is in fact arguing for psychological complexity. A comparable modern argument might say that Freud oversimplified the mechanics of the mind by setting up three arbitrary actors (Id, Ego, and Super-ego). Freudians can answer that the doctrine is not as simple as that; but the Freudianism that reached most people was fully that simplified—and Augustine might have said the same of the Manichean doctrine as that was ordinarily understood.

26.   The pestering lusts that whisper behind Augustine are imagined after the pattern of temptations in tales like Anthony's or Jerome's—the devils that would be canonized in depictions of Anthony's desert trial by Bosch and others. Their personification in this place anticipates the use Augustine will make of Anthony's story in [29].

27.   The converse of the figurative devils of the preceding paragraph is the personification of Self-Control as a figure of kind rebuke, like that of the Laws addressing Socrates in Plato's *Crito*.

28.   The biblical uses of the fig tree offer a range of possibilities of Augustine's use of it here. There are three main ones—two in the gospels (John and Matthew) and one in Genesis.

1. *Nathaniel's fig tree* (John 1.47–51). Pierre Courcelle took the fact that Augustine says he threw himself "*under* some fig tree" as proof that he was referring to the passage that says Nathaniel was "*under* a fig tree":

> Jesus saw Nathaniel approach, and said of him, "There is a true Israelite, with no trace of falsehood in him." He said it of

Nathaniel, who asked, "How do you know me?" Jesus in response said, "Even before Philip summoned you, I saw you under the fig tree." Nathaniel answered, "Rabbi, you are God's son and Israel's king." And Jesus answered: "I said I saw you under the fig, and therefore you believe? You will see far greater wonders than that." And he added: "I tell you solemnly, you will see the heavens parted, and angels rising there and returning upon the Son of Man."

Why would Augustine in the garden compare himself to Nathaniel? At a moment when he is agonizing over his debilitation by lust, it seems highly inappropriate to compare himself with "a true Israelite, with no trace of falsehood in him," who is one of the first to proclaim the divine sonship of Jesus. Augustine, in *Explaining the Psalms* 7.16, wrote: "Happy this Nathaniel, vouched for by Truth itself." Such happiness is not the note of the garden. Raymond Brown seems closer to the truth of the Johannine passage when he notes that rabbinical lore made study under the fig tree a type of observing the Law (*The Gospel According to John*, Doubleday, 1966, vol. 1, p. 87). This accords with what Augustine says of Nathaniel in *Interpreting John's Gospel* 7.17—that Nathaniel was a scholar of the Law, and therefore was not included in the apostles, who were "common men."

To accord with the use Augustine makes of the fig tree in the garden, the tree must be somehow associated with his *sin*. Some make this connection by saying that Jesus has caught Nathaniel in some evil thought—just as some think that Jesus traces in dust the sins of the would-be executioners of an adulteress (John 8.11). How would that fit with what goes before and after Jesus' remark on the fig tree—with the "true Israelite" and the proclamation? It seems more likely that Jesus was showing that he recognized Nathaniel's inmost noble aspirations, which he meant to fulfill as he recognizes the longing of others to know him—Nicodemus, for instance, at John 3.1–21 (Nicodemus is another scholar, as Augustine takes Nathaniel to be).

Another way of connecting the fig tree with sin is indicated by Augustine in *Explaining the Psalms* 31.2.9, where he says that "he was under the fig tree because he was under the fleshly condition." Similarly, at *Interpreting John's Gospel* 7.21, he says that "Nathaniel was under the fig tree as being under the shadow of death." But in both cases he explains the meaning of the fig tree in terms of the Genesis or Matthew passages discussed below—and there seems no good reason for connecting Nathaniel specifically or especially with them. The fig tree in John seems simply to indicate a unique moment Jesus identifies in one man's life. To make it general or symbolic for everyone goes against the sense of the story.

2. *The cursed fig tree* (Matthew 21.19–21).

Approaching the city in the morning, he felt hunger. Spotting one fig tree at the roadside, he went over to it, but found nothing on it but leaves. So he said, "Bear you no fruit ever!" And instantly it shriveled up. The astonished disciples asked, "How was the fig tree instantly shriveled?" Jesus spoke in answer to them: "Solemnly I tell you that, if only you have faith and doubt not, you will not only do what was done to the fig tree but if you say to a mountain, tear yourself up and throw yourself into the sea, it will do so. Pray but with belief, and all will be granted you."

Augustine and others connect this episode with sin by saying that the fig tree illustrates the moral "By your fruits you shall know them." But the fig tree is not morally to blame. Jesus is showing the power of faith. The fig tree is simply the instrument of his teaching that is at hand. It is the disciples' faith that is being challenged, not the conduct of the fig.

3. *Adam and Eve* (Genesis 2.7). The sin of Adam and Eve introduced shame in nakedness, a great concern of Augustine's: "Their eyes were opened to realize that they were naked; and they plaited fig leaves together to form loincloths." It is the shame of the body that Augustine is indicating by the way he throws himself helplessly under the fig tree. This is a way station between the nakedness "clothing" him in the public baths and the nakedness with which he goes into the healing waters of baptism to be "clothed" in Christ. The fig tree is not primarily Nathaniel's (Courcelle) or all three scriptural *topoi* (O'Donnell), but the Genesis fig tree, in line with all the other Genesis references in *The Testimony*—the tree of sin in the pear episode, the sin of Cain in the death of his friend, and the semi-Eden of the garden where he conversed with his mother.

29. Augustine presents the child's chant *Tolle! Lege!* as ambiguous or mysterious. Unlike the revelation of Self-Control, it makes him search his memory in an effort to "place" it. The fact that he fails to explain it to himself just strengthens his determination to treat it as a "sign" divinely meant for him. If he were creating a symbolic voice, as Courcelle thinks, he could have imposed an appropriate message or image. The indeterminacy of the voice is a guarantee of its factual status. A. Sizoo makes an interesting suggestion that would confirm the literal nature of the chant (*Vigiliae Christianae* 12, 1958, pp. 104–106). Since *legere* can mean "pick" or "select" as well as "read," *Tolle! Lege!* might have been a harvester's chant the child had learned, and mindlessly repeated, meaning *take* (lift) and *look* (to accept or reject the fruit or vegetable). I translate ambiguously, so the phrase can mean pick up and read (look) or pick up and evaluate.

The story of Anthony's call to be a hermit, effected by a single verse of Scripture, is now used, after having been carefully saved for this moment. The obvious place to have used it was in the story of the friends at Trier, called by the same Scripture verse to be monks. In the Latin version of the *Anthony's Life* that Augustine may have read, the story runs thus (*Vita* 2):

> With his mind mulling such things, he [Anthony] entered the church, where it chanced that the gospel was being read in which the Lord tells a rich man, "If you wish to be complete, go and sell all the possessions you have, and give the proceeds to the poor, and come, follow me, and you will have treasure in heaven." At the words, it was as if something familiar to him

before should by divine prompting be read now just for him. Recognizing the Lord's mandate, he went out at once and sold all his possessions.

The "conversion" of Alypius involves no moral anguish, since he was averse to sex—an attitude Augustine admired as a form of purity (T 6.21–22).

30. The report of the garden experience to Monnica involves what might be called persuasive congratulation. She had prayed that he become an orthodox believer, not that he become a celibate. It is true that she had opposed an early marriage for him (a thing Augustine criticized), but this was not out of a semi-incestuous possessiveness, as Rebecca West implies. She did not want him to marry "below himself." Only when he had secured a proud position at the emperor's court could she arrange a marriage with an heiress. The family had invested heavily in Augustine's career, and she expected some return on that effort. See the excellent treatment by Brent D. Shaw, "The Family in Late Antiquity" (*Past and Present* 115, 1987), pp. 33–36.

25–30. Book Eight's narrative pulse quickens as Augustine moves toward its climax. One feels this in the panting phrases, the stabbing repetitions, of his effort to prevail on his own, without grace: *modo fiat, modo fiat . . . paulo minus . . . paulo minus . . . jam jamque:*

> Make it now! Make it now! . . . I was almost there—but was not there. Still, I did not slide all the way back, but braced myself

nearby, catching my breath; then, renewing the effort, I almost made it—almost—but did not; I was all but touching, all but clasping—but no, I was not there, not yet touching, not yet clasping, not ready to die to death and live to life, still held by the engrained evil in me over the untrained good in me **[25]**.

He feels the prize slipping from him, clawing at it: *Domine, usquequo? Usquequo Domine? . . . Quamdiu guamdiu cras et cras? Quare non modo? Quare non . . .*

Lord, how much more? How much more, Lord. . . . How long, how long—on the morrow is it, always the morrow? Why never now? Why is not now . . . **[28]**.

In keeping with this quickened pace, the last and most important of the parallel conversion stories, that of Anthony, is stripped to bare-bones brevity. Elsewhere, historical presents give immediacy to the action: "of a sudden I hear . . . a voice. . . . He asks what I had read. . . . he goes beyond." The story reaches a telegraphic urgency: *Arripui, aperui, et legi* ("I snatched, opened, read"). When he goes to Monnica, asyndeton (lack of connectives) and historical presents amount to a report from the battleground: *Ingredimur, indicamus, gaudet:* "We go to [her]; speak . . . she rejoices. We give her the details of what happened. It is joy and glory to her." This is the most famous book in *The Testimony*, in large part because it is the best demonstration of Augustine's storytelling skill. It demonstrates the profit he had derived from his reading of Sallust, the moral dramatist of Roman history.

DATE DUE